In Order to Talk with the Dead

The Texas Pan American Series

In Order to Talk with the Dead

Selected Poems of Jorge Teillier

Translated and with an Introduction
by Carolyne Wright

UNIVERSITY OF TEXAS PRESS   AUSTIN

The Texas Pan American Series is published with the assistance
of a revolving publication fund established by the Pan American
Sulphur Company.

Library of Congress Cataloging-in-Publication Data

Teillier, Jorge.
    [Selections. English and Spanish]
    In order to talk with the dead : selected poems of Jorge Teillier /
selected and translated by Carolyne Wright. — 1st ed.
        p.   cm.—(The Texas Pan American series)
    English and Spanish.
    The original texts were selected from Muertes y maravillas,
Para un pueblo fantasma, and Cartas para reinas de otras
primaveras.
        ISBN 0-292-73867-6
        ISBN 0-292-78123-7 (pbk.)
        1. Teillier, Jorge—Translations into English.   I. Wright,
Carolyne, date.   II. Title.   III. Series.
    PQ8098.3.E4A29   1993
    861—dc20   92-29414

Dedicated to my parents,
Marian L. and Maurice C. Wright,
who first inspired me to study the Spanish language,
with gratitude for their encouragement,
practical assistance, and love.

CONTENTS

PART TWO

Poems from *Para un pueblo fantasma* (For a Town of Ghosts) (1978)

ACKNOWLEDGMENTS

Grateful acknowledgement is made to the following periodicals in which many of these translations first appeared:

American Poetry Review	*Massachusetts Review*
American Voice	*Mid-American Review*
Black Warrior Review	*Missouri Review*
Boulevard	*Mundus Artium*
Chelsea	*New Letters*
City Lights Review	*Ohio Review*
Cream City Review	*Organica*
Graham House Review	*Partisan Review*
Harvard Review	*Prism International*
Indiana Review	*Seattle Review*
Iowa Review	*Seneca Review*
Malahat Review	*Tampa Review*

I wish to thank the Mary Ingraham Bunting Institute of Radcliffe College; the Creative Artists Public Service (CAPS) Program of New York State; the Fine Arts Work Center in Provincetown, Massachusetts; the Fulbright Commission of Chile (through the Institute of International Education); the National Endowment for the Humanities; the Port Townsend Writers Conference; the Seattle Arts Commission; and the Corporation of Yaddo for fellowships and awards that provided support and encouragement while I was completing these translations.

For their advice, encouragement, and practical assistance at various times over the years this manuscript was in process, I wish to thank Marjorie Agosín, Jonathan Cohen, Jaime Ferrán, Jaime Giordano, Pedro Lastra, Rosa Parra Mendoza, Marcelino Peñuelas, Daniel Testa, and Jorge Teillier.

INTRODUCTION

From the Land of Nevermore:
On the Poetry of Jorge Teillier
by Carolyne Wright

My instrument to counter the world is another vision of the world . . . It's worthless to write poetry if it isn't a means by which we begin to transform ourselves.

So writes Jorge Teillier in "Sobre el mundo donde verdaderamente habito" (About the World I Really Inhabit), his Prologue to *Muertes y maravillas* (Deaths and Wonders, Santiago: Editorial Universitaria, 1971), an anthology of his selected work published between 1953 and 1970, the period of his youth and greatest poetic output. Like many other poets in the Romantic vein, Teillier found his voice early and has remained "rooted," to use his term, in the source of his poetry, the world of his childhood and youth in the rainy South of Chile:

> My poetic world was the same one I now inhabit, which I must perhaps someday destroy to preserve: the world crossed by Locomotive #245, by November clouds which make it rain at the height of summer, which are the shades of the dead who visit us, as an old aunt used to say; the world populated by mirrors which reflect not our image but that of the stranger we were, who comes from another age to meet us; the [world] where the parish bells ring and stories are still told of the founding of the town.

Such an evocative power does that world have over the poet that, even as he attempts to describe it for us in prose, he falls into the tone and rhythms of his poetry.

Appropriately enough, the poems in the first section of *Muertes y maravillas* are addressed "To the Inhabitants of the Land of Nevermore," deliberately echoing the famous refrain, "Nevermore," in

Edgar Allan Poe's poem "The Raven," and alluding to J. M. Barrie's enchanted "Never Never Land" in *Peter Pan*. But for Teillier, who believes that poetry "is a way of being and acting," to continue to dwell in the Land of Nevermore is to experience a sort of dissociation, an alienation from his ongoing adult existence in the city where he now lives and works. This alienation becomes more evident in the later poems (such as "Notes on the Author's Last Journey to the Town of His Birth"), but even his early poems are pervaded by a melancholy that seems to grow from a yearning for the lost domain of the past.

The suspended world of childhood, a time of precarious innocence, exists now only in memory, and its artifacts—the adult poet now realizes—were even then dust-covered and on the verge of evanescing. This remembered world, as evoked in Teillier's poetry, is a dreamy, small-town, rainy Chilean version of Antonio Machado's *aldea*—full of the whistles, steam plumes, and signal lanterns of the same north-south freight trains that bisect the towns and cut through the virgin forests of the Chilean *frontera* in the poetry of Pablo Neruda, Teillier's countryman and fellow *sureño*.

The *frontera* was, of course, a historical reality—Chile's own version of the North American "Far West," as Teillier calls it. As preserved in his poetry, the *frontera* is a fusion of this literal, rainy, heavily forested territory with the imagined landscapes inhabited by the autobiographical personae of Teillier's early poems: the private, oneiric Never Never Land of the pensive, bookish child of "Winter Poem" and "To a Child in a Tree," and the roaming ground of the dream-ridden, restless young man of "Afternoon in Automobile" and "Night Trains." In the cover note to *Cartas para reinas de otras primaveras*, Jorge Edwards, Chilean writer and literary critic, says that

> in Teillier's poetry there exists a mythic South, the same rainy, wooded Frontera of Pablo Neruda, but in this case rendered unreal, converted into a pretext for a verbal creation where trees, mountains, provincial village squares, are tinged with innumerable references to contemporary literature, as if literary space and that of nature were intertwined.

Having lost this mythic South—the "visionary gleam," as it were, of his childhood—the poet re-creates it in his art, giving this re-creation a super-real quality. In "Aproximaciones a la poesía de Jorge Teillier" (Approaches to the Poetry of Jorge Teillier), his introductory essay to *Muertes y maravillas*, Chilean writer Alfonso Calderón suggests an almost allegorical dimension to this process of artistic re-creation:

> The village is also an image of the universe. The overlaying of a visible landscape with the landscape of dream, and the confrontation between a paradisiacal childhood and a childhood with zones of darkness, are essential features of his lyric.

The poet is aware of this tendency, Calderón says, and as evidence he refers to a 1963 article, *"The Great Meaulnes* Turns Fifty," which Teillier wrote for *El Mercurio* of Santiago. In this article, Calderón tells us, Teillier discusses Alain Fournier's novel (translated into English as *The Lost Domain*) in which a young man discovers a seemingly enchanted house in the middle of the forest, where he falls in love with a mysterious young woman. Teillier relates this tale to the perennial human yearning for a lost or golden age, a story which in its countless variations has attained the stature of myth or archetype, because "it is this lost paradise which man knows . . . he once inhabited, without being able to find it again . . . which existed once on the earth, and whose final instance would be childhood." In another article, the poet also reminds us that childhood is not solely "the domain of purity, but [the realm where] the angels of darkness extend their wings."

This theme has been elaborated in many forms, of course: in myth, folklore, fairy tale, children's literature, and in the popular culture of the twentieth century. Teillier has taken advantage of this "scattered tradition"—as Calderón calls it—and makes frequent allusions not only to Alain Fournier's book but also to *Alice in Wonderland, Peter Pan*, and the adventure stories of Robert Louis Stevenson, as well as to the fantasy world of early motion pictures and recordings. These books and films, along with the artifacts of the poet's own past—old photo albums, sports magazines, parlor pianos, movie posters, abandoned flour mills, and country houses—are all totems from the lost era of childhood. Like Rilke, Teillier believes in the capacity of beloved objects to retain a certain power and presence by virtue of human contact, and the value which people have invested in them: they become mediums of communion with this now lost, hermetic, almost magical order of life in the past. The poet affirms that his goal is not to "encounter, as Gide has in the literal landscape, words that suggest the mystery," but to "describe the other landscape, the mysterious landscape," the contours and features of the Land of Nevermore.

Beyond the realms of myth and popular culture, the poetic influences upon Teillier have been diverse. Grandson of French settlers in Chile, he names Verlaine, Baudelaire, Mallarmé, Jules Laforgue, and Francis Jammes—whose works he has read in the original—among his poetic ancestors. He also credits the major figures of Modernism and Symbolism who wrote in his first language—Darío, Machado, and García Lorca. And he was also influenced by his fellow Chileans, both renowned and obscure: Pablo de Rokha, Rosamel del Valle, the "Baudelairean dandy" Teófilo Cid, Alberto Rojas Jiménez, Vicente Huidobro, Nicanor Parra, and the giant of them all, Pablo Neruda. Teillier refers to, and in some instances directly addresses, many of these fellow poets in his poems, as in the "Libro de homenajes" (Book of Homages) sequence. In *Animales literarios de Chile* (Literary Animals of Chile, Santiago: Ediciones Lafourcade, ca. 1981), a delightful volume of his articles reprinted from magazines, Chilean writer Enrique Lafourcade says that Teillier is widely recognized as a voracious reader, "immersing himself in Lautréamont and Jarry, in Reverdy and Apollinaire, in the Surrealists and in Jacques Prévert. All his life he has been an exceptional reader of hundreds of literary works. . . . He nourishes himself on prose writers and poets from all over the world, on histories and historians. He reads the songs of blind singers, sports magazines, oriental literatures." Lafourcade also gives us this amusing and revealing anecdote about Teillier and his Gallic heritage:

> I run into Teillier at the Book Fair not long ago. He's watching television, one of the matches of the recent World Cup of Football [soccer]. He says to me, "We're winning." I don't understand what he means, until I discover that it's France playing against some other team.

Despite the diversity of influences on Teillier and his communication, via direct address, with his literary predecessors, his work is permeated with a sense of isolation and loss. Human contact is contemplated in terms of its evanescence, and the poetry is haunted by disappearances, suspended animation, and death—preoccupations that have persisted throughout Teillier's career. The painfully lingering presence of those who are in fact absent—the mother, the beloved, the cousins and grandparents, and the cast of townspeople—is acutely felt in poems such as "Narratives," "Postcard," and "In Memory of a Closed House." Equally acute is the poet's need to recall what life was like in the childhood microcosm by walking the village's now weed-choked streets, exploring its ruined sawmills and derelict wooden bridges, and calling up memories from the time when the scene was fresh and vibrant with the speaker's sense of wonder. In poems such as "Letter of Rain" and "Afternoon Story," these journeys of memory are enhanced by the company—or imagined company—of a beloved young woman friend vanished long ago. On these return visits, Teillier's childhood village, like that of Juan Rulfo's *Pedro Páramo*, appears virtually empty of all but its ghosts: the air vibrates with the sound of disembodied voices, snatches of tunes sung by long-dead singers, and footsteps of those returning who never quite arrive—just as the poet himself can never quite arrive in his attempted imaginative returns to the past.

Curiously, only old classmates and pals from the poet's boyhood seem to remain in this village otherwise depopulated of its former inhabitants. In poems such as "One Year, Another Year," "When Everyone Goes Away," and "Notes on the Author's Last Journey . . . ," the poet joins them in their old haunts. They are either ne'er-do-wells, frittering time away in the same old bars, or upwardly mobile petit bourgeois, with dreams of getting elected to local public office and purchasing imported cars. Having stayed in their home town, these old pals serve as ambivalent indices of how far the poet has come—or how far he has strayed—from his origin, that paradise overshadowed by darkness.

Mario Benedetti, the notable Uruguayan writer, believes that Teillier's view is not as gloomy as it may appear. Quoted by Enrique Lafourcade in *Animales literarios de Chile*, Benedetti explains that

Teillier's view is tersely melancholy, but it is obvious that he does not long for any past age of the world, any lost childhood. His nostalgia is more serene, but also more plaintive than all that: it is limited to missing what man could have been in the face of the surprised, passive landscape. "The time has been too long," he says without fanfare, and we all, curiously, think about brevity, about any brevity . . .

Teillier's attitude toward the child's lost paradise may be more equivocal, in fact, than it appears. In "Golden Age," the final poem in the "Land of Nevermore" sequence, the speaker imagines a future time of unbroken happiness, in which he is reunited with his family in a resurrection of the past. The poem's dreamlike ambience is jarred, however, by an unexpected adjective in the final stanza, as everyone meets "under the solemn, *bored* gaze / of people who've never existed" (my italics). That they will meet in the logically impossible presence of people who have never existed—people who will find the family's illusions about its own supposed existence tedious—greatly compromises the validity of the speaker's and his family's metaphysical situation. The speaker then steps outside the frame of the poem to state ironically that they, and he, will only *believe*—erroneously—that they are still alive. Death is stasis, and any attempt to go back to the past creates a false life, a shadow world on the other side of time—false because it is static, because the real past was in constant flux. As is true for the figures on Keats's Grecian Urn, the irony of perpetual youth is the inability actually to live it. The price of freedom from one's "shadow and . . . name" is to have no living self with which to enjoy this return to the freedom of youth.

Death is implicit even on this side of time, immanent even in affirmations that strive, however ironically, to deny its existence—as in the repeated declaration, "Nobody's died yet in this house," that serves as a refrain in the poem of the same name. The poet, returning to the ghost town of his memory in poems such as "The Last Island" and "Signs," relives his youthful pastimes with a repetitiveness that approaches the hypnotic fixation of ritual. Like the last Buendía in the town of Macondo at the end of *One Hundred Years of Solitude*, the speaker in Teillier's poetry witnesses destruction that is inevitable, inexorable, and perhaps more real than what it destroys. The ritualization of activity here is another form of stasis within motion, a kind of death which manifests itself in the curious suspended life of these poems. In his essay "About the World I Really Inhabit," Teillier says,

> For me, poetry is the struggle against our enemy, time, and an attempt to integrate ourselves with death, of whom I was aware and to whose kingdom I have belonged since early childhood, when I sensed his footsteps climbing the steps that led to the tower of the house where I shut myself in to read. . . . Most of the people I know . . . believe that death doesn't exist or exists only for others. For this reason, childhood is present in my poems, because it is the time closest to death.

The poet's fascination with the various ways in which death is present within life is related to his explorations of the supernatural in other poems, especially "In Order to Talk with the Dead," "The Exorcisms," "Dark Lantern," and "In the Month of Foxes." The ritual actions in these poems (throwing salt on the fire, sacrificing horses, burning fruit trees in blossom) may derive from the pre-Christian beliefs and folk traditions of Hispanic and Germanic settlers in the South of Chile, or from the still-vital beliefs and practices of the indigenous Mapuche people, whose reservations and ancestral lands surround the towns of Lautaro, Teillier's birthplace, and Victoria, where he grew up. The *machis*, shamanistic priestesses and healers of the Mapuches, have never been appeased after the usurpation of their domain by the European settlers, and their presence still broods, at times threateningly, over the towns of the poet's boyhood.

All of these traditions share a sense of the power of local spirits, the numinous energy of certain objects, trees, and geological formations. Teillier has called his poetry "laric," influenced by the power of the *lares*, the household gods and local deities. In these poems, the unseen realm is superimposed on the seen; the dead mingle—sometimes indistinguishably—with the living; and the "strangers" or "outsiders" who are perpetually anticipated (in "Winter Poem," "The Exorcisms," and "Dark Lantern") may be either living or dead. Teillier uses two different words which may be translated as "stranger" or "outsider": *desconocido*, which means simply an unknown person; and the more complex *forastero*. Literally, *forastero* means "outsider" or "foreigner," but Teillier's own meaning (as he explained in a letter to me) is that of "someone who returns for a time to the town of his birth without anyone's recognizing him." This unrecognized native in the guise of an outsider, who returns again and again to the town, inspiring dread and curiosity in the boy speaker and the other inhabitants, is a projection of the poet himself. He is the adult who is opposed (as Teillier writes) "to the voice of this civilization whose meaning I reject and whose symbol is the city in which I dwell in exile, solely to earn a living, without integrating myself into it." He is the one who will come back from the living death of his present days in that city "sick with smog," to revisit his past (the death-in-life of memory, stasis, suspended animation) and to confront himself as the boy—the speaker of the early poems, fascinated and disturbed by presentiments that the stranger is a foreshadowing of his future self. This future self, who will be the adult speaker of the later poems, is the *forastero* who can never fully return.

Just as the indigenous people and their spirits have been relegated to a poverty-stricken, marginal existence, this adult speaker—the poet himself—is an outsider, not so much by external socioeconomic conditions as by personal choice. Because his values and priorities differ from those of the modern world, he is an isolated, alienated figure, both in the contemporary city he hates but depends upon for material existence (as in "Portrait of My Father, Militant Communist" and "Notes on the Author's Last Journey . . .") and in the village of the past, which gives him spiritual and creative sustenance but which no longer exists except in memory. The perpetual overlapping of time in the later poems gives them a peculiar, subtle energy. Most are written in the present tense, the author projecting himself back into the past as if he were still the youthful speaker, but a speaker with an uncanny sense that the scenes before him are long vanished. This multiple displacement—in space and time, life and death—allows the poet to invest his vision of a decaying railroad town with wonder, while acknowledging with frustration his own marginality in it.

Likewise, it is the marginal figures among his fellow poets with whom Teillier identifies, especially those poets who died young, their promise unfulfilled, often because they refused to make any practical compromise between the high and timeless ideals of their art and the exigencies of survival in the mundane modern world. Like Rosamel del Valle—to whom "The Return of Orpheus" is dedicated—the poet in contemporary society, especially one who works within the Romantic tradition, can be considered an archaic entity, a survivor from some lost age, whose art is a neglected stepchild among literary genres. For Teillier, "the poet is a marginal being, but this marginality and displacement can give birth to his greatest strength: that of transforming poetry into living experience, and of assenting to another world, beyond the sordid one in which he lives." The poet's inner conflict parallels the conflict between himself and the world, as he struggles to overcome the "mediocrity of the everyday" within himself, and to attain his true and highest self, which is one with his poetry.

These are lofty ideals, not easily realized even by the highest-minded and most disciplined of poets. Except for a few of his *homenajes* (homages), most notably "The Lost Domain," Teillier's poems are peopled with all-too-human failures. Some are casualties of the struggle between the ideal and the real; others are obscure individuals whose inner light may never have been glimpsed at all, characters whose existence was tenuous even in the quiet, small-town world of the poet's boyhood. The young speaker of Teillier's early poems observes, with curiosity and sympathy, the madwomen strolling with parasols or dancing in a lonely frenzy before their mirrors, the tramps asleep under linden trees or lighting fires in derelict sheds to warm themselves, and the drunken peasants stumbling home from the taverns. In later poems, the adult speaker identifies more closely with these characters—the tipsy postman lost on his own delivery route, his fellow patients in an alcoholic detoxification clinic outside Santiago, his fellow poets who have fled into political exile to escape the "Ogres" of military rule (as in "Now That Once Again"), while he himself has remained at home. In the fallen world of adulthood, this poet is a marginal figure, by virtue not only of his literary calling, but also of his own ordinary human struggles, especially with alcohol.

Para un pueblo fantasma, the first book of Teillier's since 1971 to contain a substantial number of recent poems, was published in 1978, during the repressive early years of the Pinochet regime. There are signs, especially in poems such as "Notes on the Author's Last Journey to the Town of His Birth," of Teillier's increasing disillusionment with his society—most notably with the deterioration of the rural and small-town life of his childhood under the onslaught of trivialized values, values which took precedence as foreign capital and consumer goods flooded back into Chile after the coup. With the arrival of television, children no longer play in the streets; local sports clubs have been superseded by distant professional teams; and the old industries and movie houses have closed for lack of business. The town is no longer a self-supporting community, but a consumer satellite of Santiago, the capital city "sick with smog." The fields filled with sunflowers, the oxcarts, the weathered wooden houses, and the unpaved roads remain; but the poet can no longer connect spiritually with them. They no longer vibrate with inner life; they are no longer the outward emblems of the boy's sense of wonder.

In *Cartas para reinas de otras primaveras*, which was published in 1985, it becomes clear that the poet has lost touch with "the glory and the dream" of his youthful creative vision, the "other vision" by which he meant to rise above the "mediocrity of the everyday." Now, preoccupied like any other petit bourgeois with his unpaid bills, seeking escape in taverns and police novels, he can hardly believe any longer in "the magic of verse." He is also tired, he says in "A Day in Madrid" (in *Para un pueblo fantasma*), of "telling stories of the provinces"—the principal subject matter of his poetry—yet in his travels he encounters only variations of the same wearisome urban and consumer-oriented themes. His days in the cities he visits are pointless rounds of small observations and details. The lines of poetry which he reads in "A Day in Madrid," and even those which his provincial Chilean poet friends send him in "Now That Once Again," seem precious and self-indulgent: he quotes them only to expose their shallowness. He yearns nevertheless for the *frontera*, but when he returns in "Notes on the Author's Last Journey . . ." as "the poet whose name appears regularly in the papers," he discovers that he is indeed a *forastero*, a native son come home a stranger ("lonely where I have never been lonely"), as he always knew and dreaded he would become. The "other vision" of his youth, which he meant to evoke in poetry, has faded; even poetry itself has become an empty form, the writing of it an empty exercise. The longing for home is futile, since he cannot go home again to a town that no longer exists as he knew it. The movement from early to later poems is a perfectly closed circle, and the speaker of these later poems confronts his own spiritual bankruptcy in landscapes which, whether new or familiar ("You have to travel so as not to travel"), all reflect stasis and suspended animation.

In a country as politicized as Chile, the question of a writer's views inevitably arises, even for a generally nonpolitical poet such as Teillier. During the three-year presidency of Salvador Allende, when Teillier published his collection of new and selected poems, *Muertes y maravillas*, humanitarian and socialist values were the norm in literature. Among Popular Unity supporters and sympathizers, these values were sine qua non, and anyone involved in public life had to come to grips with his or her own political orientation. This process of self-examination also occurred among those in the arts, especially among writers, who worked in the shadow of 1971 Nobel Prize winner and idealistic Communist Party member, Pablo Neruda.

"Neruda was the poetic hero of my generation," Teillier writes in "About the World I Really Inhabit." This was especially true in 1953, when, like other boys from the provinces (including the young Neruda himself some thirty years earlier), Teillier made the "soot-baptized journey" by train to Santiago to attend the University of Chile. By then, Neruda had served his country as a diplomat and a senator, had fled Chile in disguise across the Andes to escape the arrest order of the formerly leftist president González Videla, and had written his masterwork, *Canto general*. According to Teillier, Neruda was at that time lamenting the fact that young people were still reading his difficult, surrealistic early collection, *Residencia en la tierra*. Neruda called to younger poets to speak "with simple words to the simple man, and in the name of socialist realism . . . to build socialism." But, Teillier admits,

I was unable to write . . . political or "socialist realist" poetry. Son of a Communist, descendant of artisans and small farmers, I knew in a sentimental way that poetry should be an instrument of struggle and liberation, and my earliest poet friends were those who were at that time following the example of Neruda. But [my inability to do the same] created in me a sense of guilt that even now habitually pursues me. I could easily be regarded as a decadent poet, but it seems to me that poetry cannot be subordinated to any ideology. . . . No poetry has alleviated hunger or remedied social injustice, but its beauty can help us to survive hardship. I have written what was dictated by my truest self, the one I try to reach in this struggle between myself and my poetry. Because what matters is not . . . writing good or bad verse, but transforming oneself into a poet, overcoming the mediocrity of the everyday . . . in order to go on listening to Keats's nightingale, which gives joy forever.

This was Teillier's statement on his relationship to political poetry in "About the World I Really Inhabit," which was written in late 1968, during the Christian Democratic presidency of Eduardo Frei. At that time, momentum was building in Chile for a speedier process of social change, for more effective land reform policies, and for independence from the influence of foreign-owned businesses on domestic policy. This momentum culminated in the election of Salvador Allende and his Popular Unity coalition in September 1970. Teillier's *Muertes y maravillas*, which included as its prologue the essay cited above, was published in August 1971, during that brief period when the arts and literature of all political viewpoints flourished in Chile—a renaissance of sorts which was abruptly curtailed by the military coup of September 1973.

Besides the prose passage quoted, *Muertes y maravillas* contained only one poem that overtly referred to politics: "Portrait of My Father, Militant Communist." This poem—dated 1961, well before the Allende years—is a fond and admiring recollection of Teillier's father Fernando, whose union-organizing efforts among the rural poor in the South of Chile put his life at risk in the 1930's, and whose Communist Party membership sent him into exile after the 1973 coup. Whatever his father's political convictions, Teillier was not forced to flee Chile on the basis of this poem or the few socialist references in the long narrative sequences "Crónica del forastero" and "Treinta años después" (not translated here) with which *Muertes y maravillas* ends—possibly because these poems alluded to bygone events and did not call readers to take any political action in the present. After the coup, Teillier kept his political views out of the public record, and except for trips to Spain and to Peru to visit his daughter and her family, he remained in Chile. It is noteworthy, however, that *Para un pueblo fantasma*, published in 1978, reprinted only eight of the ten poems included in the "Book of Homages" section of the earlier volume. One of the two poems omitted from the newer, expanded section of the same name was "Portrait of My Father, Militant Communist."

Despite Teillier's perceived nonpolitical stance, as declared in his 1968 essay, many of his later poems contain images and passing comments that refer to social and economic conditions in Chile during the Pinochet regime. The inclusion of such oblique and ironic protests is not the same as writing in a deliberately revolutionary or "socialist realist" mode, but these poems cannot be called entirely nonpolitical either. Their realism is based on the poet's individual observations and responses, rather than on any preconceived ideological framework. No longer buffered by the uplifting vision evident in his earlier work, Teillier was personally affected—as was everyone in Chile—by the official lies and ongoing threat of violence in the regime. His health problems rendered him more vulnerable, and he treats these with fierce irony in "Clinical Landscape," referring to himself as "the poet in residence," and sketching verbally the various private dramas in which his fellow patients in the alcoholism treatment clinic are trapped. The clinic is portrayed as a microcosm of the society outside: the paranoia which prevails within its walls reflects the paranoia rampant in the police state. A flock of thrushes, alighting momentarily in trees next to the barbed-wire fence, is suspected of transmitting clandestine messages. The only patient allowed outside to purchase the pro-government newspaper is both "a hopeless madman" and a "descendant of Germans"—in a country to which hundreds of ex-Nazis and Nazi sympathizers fled to resettle after World War II. In the madness of right-wing repression, who else could make the correct selection of reading material with the proper attitude? Wasted, self-destructive lives go on here, watched over by the blue plaster Virgin, protected by "saints" who bear the names of tranquilizing drugs. It is a bitter picture, but the harshness of tone is appropriate in a world where beautiful poems with beautiful subject matter seem less and less credible.

This harsh voice finds further expression in poems included in *Cartas para reinas de otras primaveras*, as Teillier implicates himself in his oblique accusations against his country. In "Everything's Gone White," his own double dresses in black and becomes a demonic figure who could be vampire or executioner, pulling on gloves

which the Prince of Lies hands to his disciples
so they can strangle themselves
without the aid of the foreigners who betrayed them. . . .

Could these lines allude to the covert participation of outside inter-
ests in the 1973 coup, and to many Chileans' complicity in the con-
tinuation of the military regime? This book was published in 1985,
in a period when Pinochet was restoring some freedom of expression
in an attempt to improve his image at home and abroad. The poet
appears to take advantage of this freedom, in a number of increas-
ingly overt political allusions.

In "Now That Once Again," Teillier evokes the atmosphere of lin-
gering dread that predominated in the years following the coup.
With his descriptions of the prowling radio-patrol cars and the Lieu-
tenant of the Guard with "his little moustache of an apprentice /
Nazi," Teillier insinuates a parallel between this state and Hitler's
Germany. The poet is consigned to a wintry urban wasteland full
of "godforsaken lovers," homeless "drifters and drunks" who sneak
into churches to sleep, and gangs of boys "hostile to the outsider."
Again the *frontera* is far away, and the poet, alone with his books
and memories, empathizes with all who seem as marginal in their
own way as he feels. He muses about his "brothers" in exile, and his
decision to light the fire at the poem's end is both a literal response
to the winter cold and a symbolic act demonstrating his determina-
tion for some sort of social action.

The most powerful poem representing this phase of Teillier's work
is "No Sign of Life." The title could be an allusion to the colloquial
Chilean term for a political reactionary, a *momio*—akin to *momia*,
"mummy"—someone whose human sympathies are dead. Or it
could simply highlight the paralysis of will and initiative which
overwhelmed many in the Pinochet police state after September
1973. Careful attention to self-censorship and constant vigilance
over one's words and actions—these are survival mechanisms such
as George Orwell, Czeslaw Miloscz, and other writers on totali-
tarian regimes have described. Under such conditions, Teillier says,
"one must speak in an undertone," and even to slurp the soup at an
official dinner is to betray publicly, dangerously, our true hopes.
Those who wish to stay out of trouble must "learn to behave" them-
selves because in the Pinochet regime, as in many dictatorships,
citizens were encouraged to inform on friends, neighbors, and family
members. Such denunciations became a way to settle old scores or
to seek one's own political advantage at the expense of others, as
well as a means for those in power to keep everyone divided. No
one, in such a state, could trust anyone else. Allusions to the reign
of terror that followed the coup are not disguised in this poem—
even in the ironically negative assurance that "never again will
blood run in the streets," or in the poet's mention of the instructions

to jettison banned "leftist" books and recordings, which many Chileans destroyed or concealed in fear of the soldiers' house-to-house searches for any incriminating pro-Allende material. Teillier's sarcasm is blatant in his ostensible praise of the "time of austerity" after the failure of some of Pinochet's economic measures of the late 1970's:

> Wives sing happily
> while they mend the only suit
> of their laid-off husbands.

Teillier also seems to insinuate that government officials and other beneficiaries of Pinochet's regime are rodents consuming the scanty supplies of cheese in the name of a future plenty they are doing nothing to foster. In such a situation, there is not much hope of speedy recovery from any of the national ills.

All of these references emerge as part of the poet's "desperate song" of love that is not so much lost as rendered pointless, in which even remembering the beloved becomes an "act of despair or elegance," and the only "sacrament" remaining in the debased contemporary world is not any rite of passage through life, but suicide. In the society depicted in the poem, genuine love is impossible; only violent, dangerous acts, such as derailing trains or violating curfew, have any impact. The closest that lovers can come to communicating is to make "sun signals . . . with the hand mirror"—like the "clandestine messages" of thrushes in "Clinical Landscape"—but such limited communication is far from fulfilling for human beings. The poet retreats into alcohol and Salvation Army literature, and announces, as if the news were good, that syphilis "will once again be incurable"—perhaps as an ironic reflection of sentiments held by those who believe that syphilis is a just punishment for sins of the flesh. Similarly, he declares, almost triumphantly, that children can dream of taking up careers which have now become truly lucrative and admired—as "economists or dictators." The cynicism of these lines is a far cry from the tenuous idealism expressed by many artists, writers, and political figures during the Allende years; the irony and even sarcasm evident here are certainly far removed from the fragile "world of innocence" of the poet's youth.

Sadly fallen though the world of these later poems may be, they are enriched by Teillier's embrace of more of the miscellany of culture and the events of recent history than is found in his earlier work, and by the sometime clashing interaction of different dictions and degrees of irony, along with flashes of his earlier lyricism. This mixed style is akin to what Ernesto Cardenal has called *exteriorismo*:

> ... poetry created with images from the world around us [*el mundo exterior*], ... an objective poetry: narrative and anecdotal, made with elements from real life, with concrete things, proper names and precise details, exact dates and figures and facts and statements.

Whether or not Teillier's style continues to evolve in this "exteriorist" mode remains to be seen. Certainly his poetry has developed in a more narrative, anecdotal direction, and it took on a political dimension at precisely the time when most Chilean writers who worked in this vein prior to September 1973 were in exile. Teillier stayed in Chile: he was able to witness the full trajectory of the Pinochet regime. His own tendency to dwell on people and events from the vanished past parallels the obsessive recollection of fellow Chileans who lost family members to the summary executions, the disappearances, and the years in exile. Many of these "vanished friends" who survived have gradually returned to Chile, following the return to democracy marked by the December 1989 election and the March 1990 swearing-in of Christian Democrat Patricio Aylwin to the presidency. It will be interesting to see what effect the new national atmosphere will have upon Teillier and his personal forms of poetic witness and recollection.

Note. The quotation from Ernesto Cardenal is from the Introduction to *With Walker in Nicaragua* (Middleton, Conn.: Wesleyan University Press, 1984). The translation is by Jonathan Cohen. All other quotations of writings by Jorge Teillier and others are translated by Carolyne Wright.

TRANSLATOR'S NOTE

I first encountered the poetry of Jorge Teillier in late 1971, in the bookstore of the Universidad de Chile on the Avenida Bernardo O'Higgins in downtown Santiago. As part of my project for the 1971–1972 Fulbright Study Grant which brought me to Chile, I had proposed to undertake translation of work by contemporary Chilean poets. Just before my departure from the United States, I had acquired a small, representative volume, *Chile: An Anthology of New Writing* (Kent, Ohio: Kent State University Press, 1970), edited by Miller Williams, which contained a few translated poems by each of several younger Chilean poets. Professor Hugo Montes of the Universidad Católica, who was teaching a course in Latin American literature which I audited in late 1971, had suggested some additional names. Once every week or ten days, armed with these two lists, I haunted the dusty display tables of the Librería Universitaria. On one of these visits, I brought away a bright blue paperback copy of *Muertes y maravillas*, Teillier's volume of new and selected poems, recently published by the Editorial Universitaria in its "Letras del sur" series.

Pablo Neruda had just won the Nobel Prize for Literature a few weeks earlier. The morning after the announcement, windows of every bookstore in Santiago were plastered with banners proclaiming "PABLO NERUDA PREMIO NOBEL 1971"—and the prices of all volumes by Neruda had doubled. (Neruda himself was in Paris, as Cultural Attaché for the Chilean Embassy to France; he did not return to Chile until after I had departed.) Despite guaranteed publisher interest for any volume of Neruda translation, I had already seen enough of these, by various renowned translators, dominating the Poetry-in-Translation shelves of bookstores back home. This was just at the beginning of the "Boom," as critics called it: the sudden surge, in North America and Europe, in the popularity of Latin American literature in translation. If Neruda was already over-represented even before winning the Nobel Prize, I thought, how many more translators would now descend upon the body of his work? I did not want to find myself unknowingly duplicating the efforts of several others.

Gabriela Mistral—now the *other* Chilean winner of the Nobel

Prize for Literature, despite having received her award in 1945, twenty-six years before Neruda—was also suggested to me. Her work had been translated, but so far not extensively. For my birthday in July 1971, my mother had given me a lovely volume, the *Selected Poems of Gabriela Mistral* (Baltimore: Johns Hopkins University Press, 1971), a bilingual edition translated and edited by Doris Dana, with woodcut illustrations by Antonio Frasconi. I was impressed by Mistral's profound spirituality and love for humanity, by the depth of sorrow in her majestic and lonely verses, by their complex and subtle patterns of rhyme and meter. I had even made a pilgrimage of sorts, in October 1971, to the village of Montegrande in the Elqui Valley where she had spent her childhood. But I was not ready to tackle such spare and solitary verses: it would have been like trying to translate Emily Dickinson into Spanish. Besides, Mistral's work already had a highly knowledgeable advocate in translator Doris Dana, the late poet's devoted friend and literary executrix.

I resolved to find a living Chilean poet, whose work was substantial but not yet well represented in English translation, a poet whose idiom was contemporary and compatible with my own. My own poetry writing was in its fledgling phase, and I wanted to translate the work of someone from whom I could learn more about the writing of poetry—much as I did from simply reading Neruda or Vallejo or the contemporary North American poets—and someone with whom I might be able to correspond. I pored through the collections I purchased at the Librería Universitaria.

Perhaps because his number was listed in the Santiago telephone directory, I simply rang up poet Enrique Lihn one morning, introduced myself in my still-halting, overly correct Spanish, and told him I was impressed with his poetry and interested in translating a selection for publication in the United States. He seemed to assent to my request, because we made an appointment to meet at the same Librería where I had purchased his books—an appropriately literary and neutral place, I thought. I don't recall anyone's giving me Lihn's number, or recommending to me that I contact him. It would not have occurred to me to ask Professor Montes or any of my handful of intellectual acquaintances to mention my name to Lihn, or to arrange an introduction. At twenty-two, having barely emerged from undergraduate studies in which I viewed poets as cultural colossi—more like Corinthian columns than accomplished but fallible fellow human beings—I had no idea how to comport myself in the grown-up world of literary networking. My audacity, born of ignorance, was a glaring exception to my usual shyness around anyone over thirty. Sr. Lihn may have sensed some of this, and I should not have been surprised when he failed to show up for our appointment.

At least, I *think* he failed to show up. As I drifted between the tables and shelves, through dust motes swirling in the late-afternoon shafts of light falling from the high windows, I did not ask any of the clerks if they espied poet Enrique Lihn. I did not approach any of the few over-thirty male browsers to enquire if one of them was the gentleman in question. None of these browsers appeared to be looking around curiously for a young *gringa* Fulbright Scholar. Several hours after the time of our supposed appointment, I slunk home. My brief moment of boldness having passed, I did not call Sr. Lihn to reschedule, nor did I ever translate any of his poems. That was also the end of my attempts to meet the poets whose books I was acquiring. I spent the rest of my time in Chile traveling, study-ing lithography and copper-plate etching, listening to the musicians of the New Song movement at the folk club "La Peña de los Parra," reading Latin American novels and poetry in the original Spanish and—later—Portuguese, and becoming as close to bilingual in Chi-lean Spanish as I could.

It was in the fall of 1973, while I was at Syracuse University work-ing on a master's degree in Creative Writing, that I first translated a Teillier poem, "Para hablar con los muertos," which would subse-quently give this collection its title. The recent coup in Chile had sent me back to my boxes of Chilean books: I realized that many of these volumes, published by the Universidad de Chile and other pro-Allende houses, had no doubt been destroyed or "disappeared" within Chile. Although I had not contacted Teillier and did not know what his situation was, I felt that translation of his work would be one small act of preservation. The dreamlike, small-town, rainy ambience of his *Muertes y maravillas* poems appealed to me, a young poet from Seattle whose earliest influences were the works of Madeline DeFrees, Richard Hugo, Carolyn Kizer, Theodore Roethke, William Stafford, David Wagoner, and others of the North-west school. And my own travels to the South of Chile—to Puerto Montt, the Lake Llanquihue region, Concepción, Arauco, and Te-muco, which were all regions similar in geography and atmosphere to my native Pacific Northwest—made Teillier's poetic world very familiar. So I was pleased when some of my earliest translation ef-forts were published in the *Malahat Review* and a few other maga-zines; and I included a group of these early Teillier translations in the manuscript of my master's thesis.

In 1977 and 1978, under Dr. Daniel Testa of Syracuse University's Department of Romance Languages, I worked on more of these translations as part of an independent project for the Doctor of Arts in Creative Writing. But then the demands of examinations, dissertation preparation, and—after the degree—several short-term teaching positions, caused me to put Teillier's poems aside until a 1980–1981 Writing Fellowship took me to the Fine Arts Work Center in Provincetown, Massachusetts, where I was able to resume this work. By the late spring of 1984, after living for several months in New Orleans, I had finished most of the translations I intended to do from *Muertes y maravillas*. While on a short reading tour of Long Island, I had the good fortune to get an address for Teillier in Chile from Professors Jaime Giordano and Pedro Lastra of the Romance Languages Department of SUNY at Stony Brook, both of whom encouraged me to contact the poet and to complete a volume of translations of his poems.

I wrote to the address given, and was cheered to receive an enthusiastic and detailed response from Teillier, commenting on the examples of work I had sent, and giving me wholehearted permission to pursue the project and to publish the translations both in magazines and in book form. This was the beginning of a two-year correspondence, in which Teillier made many valuable suggestions, clarified the meanings of several regional terms—as well as his own private meanings for some words—and kept me informed of his addresses, which were changing almost as often as my own was. While on a visiting appointment at Whitman College in 1984–1985, I obtained a copy of *Para un pueblo fantasma*, by then out of print, through interlibrary loan. When it was published in 1985, Teillier sent me a copy of his most recent book, *Cartas para reinas de otras primaveras*. He also provided me with photocopies of a few of his poems which had been published in 1968 in *Triquarterly*, in translations by Margaret Sayers Peden. During a five-week residency at Yaddo that year, I completed drafts of most of the rest of the poems included here, revised my earliest efforts from the 1970's, and resumed submission of these efforts to literary journals. They appeared in *American Poetry Review, American Voice, Black Warrior Review, Graham House Review, Iowa Review, Seneca Review,* and other magazines in rather rapid succession.

By 1986, I had almost completed *In Order to Talk with the Dead* to my satisfaction; but a 1986–1987 Indo-U.S. Subcommission Fellowship took me to Calcutta, India, on an altogether different undertaking—the study and translation of work by contemporary Bengali women poets and writers. During this time, I lost contact with Teillier. There was no reply to the letters I sent in the months before departing for India, but when I returned home, I determined to try

again. After spending nearly two years in Calcutta, and while antici-
pating departure on a Fulbright Research Grant to Bangladesh the
following year, I knew it was "now or never" that I had to fulfill my
commitment to Teillier's poetry. I revised the remaining drafts from
the later books, and continued my attempts to communicate with
the poet.

By happy chance, a family friend, Rosa Parra Mendoza, was plan-
ning a visit in March 1989 to her relatives still in Chile, and she was
able to carry letters and a copy of the completed manuscript with
her. These she delivered to Teillier's address in Santiago, after find-
ing a directory listing and speaking with him by telephone. Al-
though his voice was very faint, she told me later, he sounded
pleased about the manuscript. Unfortunately, he would be away for
several days, he said, so she was not able to meet him on the day she
brought the packet to his house. Nevertheless, I was glad to learn
that "the elusive Sr. Teillier" was still in favor of the project, and
that a copy of the working manuscript was now in his possession.

While continuing to send groups of translations to literary maga-
zines, I had begun to submit the completed manuscript, by the fall
of 1988, to publishers. I was already in Dhaka, Bangladesh, occupied
with the second phase of the Bengali translation project, when I re-
ceived the long-distance call on Christmas Eve 1989 from my
family, informing me that the University of Texas Press had ac-
cepted *In Order to Talk with the Dead*.

In this collection, I have tried to provide a generous representative
selection of Teillier's poetry, from his earliest to most recent pe-
riods. Included are many of the shorter lyrical poems from *Muertes
y maravillas*, from his series entitled "To the Inhabitants of the
Land of Nevermore"—a body of lyrical work in the Romantic tradi-
tion that is probably definitive now, as his style has evolved toward
the "exteriorist" mode, especially in the longer and more anecdotal
narrative poems. I have also translated a number of these longer
poems, such as the early "Story of a Prodigal Son" and "Night
Trains," in which the poet's voice still evokes the lyrical mode and
takes as subject matter his recollections from the lost domain of his
childhood. From his two most recent books, *Para un pueblo fan-
tasma* and *Cartas para reinas de otras primaveras*, I have included
a number of shorter poems in a lyrical mode, as well as longer nar-
rative works such as "Clinical Landscape," "Notes on the Author's
Last Journey to the Town of His Birth," "Now That Once Again,"
and "No Sign of Life." These poems are arranged according to their
sequence in the volumes in which they originally appeared, under

section headings derived from the original volumes' titles and sections. The only difficulty with this method of organization was that the "Libro de homenajes" (Book of Homages) section appeared twice: in *Muertes y maravillas,* and also in *Para un pueblo fantasma,* with some omissions (such as "Portrait of My Father, Militant Communist") and the addition of several new poems in the later book. I decided to place this section according to its sequence in *Para un pueblo fantasma,* with "So Long" (which is included in both books) as the final poem in the section, as it appeared in the 1978 volume. This arrangement does take "Portrait of My Father, Militant Communist" out of its original sequence, but Teillier gave the poem a composition date of 1961, which anchors it firmly in the chronology of his poetic development. The composition date may also indicate that its initial appearance in *Muertes y maravillas* was already out of sequence with respect to Teillier's oeuvre, since it was written so much earlier, but not published until the 1971 volume. I also felt that including the "Book of Homages" section with the *Para un pueblo fantasma* poems would give this book a better-balanced arrangement, especially since the poet himself saw fit to reprint the section in an expanded form in his 1978 collection.

I have elected not to translate some of his longest, most anecdotal poems (such as "Crónica del forastero" and "Treinta años después" from *Muertes y maravillas;* "Cosas vistas" and "El osario de los inocentes" from *Para un pueblo fantasma;* and "Paseos con Carolina" and "Viaje de invierno" from *Cartas para reinas de otras primaveras*) for reasons of space. Moreover, many of the cultural and historical allusions which Teillier makes in these poems are so particularly Chilean that the English-speaking, non-Chilean reader would feel excluded from any immediate grasp of their import. Although a few of the poems published here warranted some notes as background for the reader of English, I have tried to avoid excessive footnoting. There are, however, another dozen poems which I had translated from the two most recent books and which I hoped to include in this collection. Unfortunately, because of the immense difficulties involved in corresponding with the Chilean publishers, and technicalities in the way permission to reprint was obtained, I have had to exclude these poems from the present volume. Nevertheless, this collection as it stands is meant to serve as a comprehensive, definitive introduction to Teillier's selected poems in English translation, to give exposure to all phases of his poetic development.

My goal in translation has been to create English renderings which are both faithful to the original Spanish and successful as poems in English—as if they had been written in English in the first place. I have tried to respect the original diction, syntax, and integrity of line—as well as the mood—of each poem, and also achieve a natural quality in the target language, English. Fortunately, with Teillier's work these effects have not been too difficult to achieve, because his imagery tends to be quite concrete, his phrasing lends itself readily to American English, and the realm of European and American literature and popular culture from which he draws many of his allusions will be familiar to most readers of English. For terms and usages that are specifically Chilean, unique to the *frontera*, or peculiar to the poet himself, I am grateful to Sr. Teillier for his comments and suggestions, as I am for his permission and encouragement for this project.

Note. The translations in this volume are derived from Teillier's anthology of new and selected work, *Muertes y maravillas* (Santiago: Editorial Universitaria de Chile, 1971), and from his two most recent collections, *Para un pueblo fantasma* (Valparaíso: Ediciones Universitarias de Valparaíso, 1978) and *Cartas para reinas de otras primaveras* (Santiago: Ediciones Manieristas, 1985). As of this writing, all of these books are out of print.

PART ONE

Poems from *Muertes y maravillas*
(Deaths and Wonders)
(1953–1971)

Otoño secreto

Cuando las amadas palabras cotidianas
pierden su sentido
y no se puede nombrar ni el pan,
ni el agua, ni la ventana,
y ha sido falso todo diálogo que no sea
con nuestra desolada imagen,
aún se miran las destrozadas estampas
en el libro del hermano menor,
es bueno saludar los platos y el mantel puestos sobre la mesa,
y ver que en el viejo armario conservan su alegría
el licor de guindas que preparó la abuela
y las manzanas puestas a guardar.

Cuando la forma de los árboles
ya no es sino el leve recuerdo de su forma,
una mentira inventada
por la turbia memoria del otoño,
y los días tienen la confusión
del desván a donde nadie sube
y la cruel blancura de la eternidad
hace que la luz huya de sí misma,
algo nos recuerda la verdad
que amamos antes de conocer:
las ramas se quiebran levemente,
el palomar se llena de aleteos,
el granero sueña otra vez con el sol,
encendemos para la fiesta
los pálidos candelabros del salón polvoriento
y el silencio nos revela el secreto
que no queríamos escuchar.

From *A los habitantes del País de Nunca Jamás*
(To the Inhabitants of the Land of Nevermore)
(1953–1970)

Secret Autumn

When the beloved everyday words
lose their sense,
and we can't give a name to bread,
or water, or windows,
and all dialogue not with our own
abandoned image has been false,
we can still look at the ruined prints
in our little brother's book;
it's good to greet the plates and linen set upon the table,
to see that in the old cabinet
the cherry cordial our grandmother made
and the apples put by for storage
still keep their joy.

When the trees' form
is no more than the slightest recollection,
a lie invented
by the troubled memory of autumn,
and the days are disordered
as the attic nobody climbs to,
and the cruel whiteness of eternity
makes light flee from itself,
something reminds us of the truth
that we love before knowing:
branches break gently,
the dovecote fills with flutterings,
the granary dreams once again of sun,
for the party we light
pale candelabras in the dusty salon,
and silence reveals to us the secret
we didn't want to hear.

Alegría

Centellean los rieles
pero nadie piensa en viajar.
De la sidrería viene olor
a manzanas recién molidas.
Sabemos que nunca estaremos solos
mientras haya un puñado de tierra fresca.

La llovizna es una oveja compasiva
lamiendo las heridas
hechas por el viento de invierno.
La sangre de las manzanas
ilumina la sidrería.

Desaparece la linterna roja
del último carro del tren.
Los vagabundos duermen
a la sombra de los tilos.
A nosotros nos basta mirar
un puñado de tierra en nuestras manos.

Es bueno beber un vaso de cerveza
para prolongar la tarde.
Recordar el centelleo de los rieles.
Recordar la tristeza
dormida como una vieja sirvienta
en un rincón de la casa.
Contarles a los amigos desaparecidos
que afuera llueve en voz baja
y tener en las manos
un puñado de tierra fresca.

Joy

The rails glimmer
but no one thinks of traveling.
The smell of newly pressed apples
drifts from the cider mill.
We know we'll never be alone
as long as a handful of fresh earth remains.

The rain-mist is a merciful sheep
licking the wounds
made by the wind of winter.
Blood of apples
lights up the cider mill.

The red lantern vanishes
on the last car of the train.
Tramps sleep in shade
of the linden trees.
For us it's enough to gaze
at a handful of earth in our hands.

It's good to drink a glass of beer
to prolong the afternoon.
To remember the glimmer of rails.
To remember sorrow
asleep like an old servant
in a corner of the house.
To tell our friends who've vanished
that outside it's raining in a low voice
and to hold in our hands
a handful of fresh earth.

La última isla

De nuevo vida y muerte se confunden
como en el patio de la casa
la entrada de las carretas
con el ruido del balde en el pozo.
De nuevo el cielo recuerda con odio
la herida del relámpago,
y los almendros no quieren pensar
en sus negras raíces.

El silencio no puede seguir siendo mi lenguaje,
pero sólo encuentro esas palabras irreales
que los muertos les dirigen a los astros y a las hormigas,
y de mi memoria desaparecen el amor y la alegría
como la luz de una jarra de agua
lanzada inútilmente contra las tinieblas.

De nuevo sólo se escucha
el crepitar inextinguible de la lluvia
que cae y cae sin saber por qué,
parecida a la anciana solitaria que sigue
tejiendo y tejiendo;
y se quiere huir hacia un pueblo
donde un trompo todavía no deja de girar
esperando que yo lo recoja,
pero donde se ponen los pies
desaparecen los caminos,
y es mejor quedarse inmóvil en este cuarto
pues quizás ha llegado el término del mundo,
y la lluvia es el estéril eco de ese fin,
una canción que tratan de recordar
labios que se deshacen bajo tierra.

The Last Island

Once again life and death get mixed up
like the rattle of oxcarts
coming into the courtyard
with the bucket's clank in the well.
Once again the sky recalls with hatred
the lightning's wound,
and the almond trees don't want to think
about their black roots.

Silence can't go on being my native tongue,
but I only find those unreal words
that the dead address to stars and ants,
and love and joy disappear from my memory
like light from a water jar
flung vainly at the shadows.

Once again one hears only
the incessant spatter of rain
that falls and falls without knowing why,
like the lonely old crone who goes on
knitting and knitting;
and one wants to flee to a town
where a top won't stop spinning
till I pick it up;
but where one's feet step
the roads disappear,
and it's better to stay put in this room
for maybe the end of the world has come,
and the rain is its barren echo,
a song that lips dissolving
under the earth try to remember.

Imagen para un estanque

Y así pasan las tardes:
silenciosas, como gastadas monedas
en manos de avaros.
Y yo escribo cartas que nunca envío
mientras los manzanos se extinguen
víctimas de sus propias llamas.

Hasta que de lejos
vienen las voces
de ventanas golpeadas por el viento
en las casas desiertas,
y pasan bueyes desenyugados
que van a beber al estero.
Entonces debo pedirle al tiempo
un recuerdo que no se deforme
en el turbio estanque de la memoria.

Y horas que sean
reflejos de sol
en el dedal de la hermana,
crepitar de la leña
quemándose en la chimenea
y claros guijarros
lanzados al río por un ciego.

He confiado en la noche

He confiado en la noche
pues durante ella amo la vida,
así como los pájaros
aman la muerte a la salida del sol.
Pero la noche
no es sino una brizna de pasto
volando al resoplido de un potrillo,
y a la luz desigual del fuego de leña

Image for a Pond

And so the afternoons go by:
silent, like spent coins
in the hands of misers.
And I write letters I never send
while the apple trees are extinguished,
victims of their own flames.

Until from afar
the voices come
of windows buffeted by wind
in the abandoned houses,
and unyoked oxen go by
on their way to the inlet to drink.
Then I must ask of time
a recollection that won't be distorted
in memory's turbid pond.

And hours that are
reflections of sun
on the sister's thimble,
crackle of firewood
burning in the fireplace
and clear pebbles
flung by a blind man into the river.

I Have Trusted in the Night

I have trusted in the night
because I love life then
as birds
love death at the rising of the sun.
But night
is no more than a grass blade
flying at the snorting of a colt,
and by the campfire's uneven light

veo que sólo me queda el terror del gusano
sintiendo el trueno en la gota de agua,
la tempestad en la caída de las agujas del castaño.

Relatos

I

El vuelo de las aves
es un canto recién aprendido por la tierra.
El día entra en la casa
como un perro mojado de rocío.

Mira: se encienden las hogueras de los gallos.
Los cazadores preparan sus morrales.
Los caballos los esperan
rompiendo con sus cascos
el cielo que apenas pesa
sobre lagunas de escarcha.

Tú eres un sueño que no recordamos
pero que nos hace despertar alegres.
Una ventana abierta hacia el trigo maduro.
Busquemos grosellas junto al cerco
cuyos hombros abruman los cerezos silvestres.

II

Un viento de otra estación se lleva la mañana.
Huyes hacia tu casa
cuando el viento dobla los pinos
de las orillas del río.
Ya no quedan grosellas.
¿Por qué no vuelven los cazadores
que vimos partir esta mañana?
Tú quieres que nunca haya sucedido nada
y en la buhardilla abres un baúl
para vestirte como novia de otro siglo.

I see that all I have left is the terror of the worm
sensing thunder in the drop of water,
storm in the chestnut catkin's fall.

Narratives

I
The flight of birds
is a song recently learned by the earth.
Day comes into the house
like a dog soaked with dew.

Look: the roosters' fires are kindled.
Hunters get their gamebags ready.
Their horses wait,
breaking with their hooves
the sky that hardly weighs anything
over frost-covered ponds.

You're a dream we don't remember
but which makes us wake up happy.
A window open on ripe wheat.
Let's look for gooseberries by the fence
whose shoulders overwhelm the wild cherry trees.

II
Wind from another season carries off the morning.
You flee toward your house
when wind bends pine trees
on the riverbanks.
No gooseberries left.
Why don't they return, the hunters
we watched depart this morning?
You want nothing ever to have happened
and in the garret, open a trunk
to dress like a bride from another century.

III

El abandono silba llamando a sus amigos.
La noche y el sueño
amarran sus caballos frente a las ventanas.
El dueño de casa baja a la bodega
a buscar sidra guardada desde el año pasado.
Se detiene el reloj de péndulo.
Clavos oxidados
caen de las tablas.
El dueño de casa demora demasiado
—quizás se ha quedado dormido entre los toneles—.

Una mañana busqué grosellas al fondo del patio.
En la tarde este mismo viento
luchaba con los pinos a orillas del río.
Se detienen los relojes.
Oigo pasos de cazadores que quizás se han muerto.
De pronto no somos sino un puñado de sombras
que el viento intenta dispersar.

Tarde

La tarde es una canción
a veces tarareada
por un viajero solitario.
Cuando la canción se apaga
el viento trae palabras
que los árboles no comprenden.

Hojas miedosas se refugian en los cuartos.
Ellas huyen del árbol lleno de musgo,
ese brujo que ha pactado con la noche
y nos ordena cerrar las ventanas.

Toque de queda en el cuartel. Mis amigos
dejan de hacer tagüitas en el río.
¿A qué viajero que una vez cantaba
aún siguen esperando en este pueblo?

III
Neglect whistles, calling to its friends.
Night and dream
tie their horses before the windows.
The master of the house goes down to the wine cellar
to look for last year's cider.
The grandfather clock stops.
Rusted nails
fall from the boards.
The master of the house delays too long—
perhaps he's fallen asleep between the casks.

One morning I looked for gooseberries at the far end of the
    courtyard.
That afternoon the same wind
fought with pines on the riverbank.
The clocks stop.
I hear the footsteps of hunters who perhaps are dead.
Suddenly we're no more than a handful of shadows
the wind intends to scatter.

Afternoon

The afternoon is a song
hummed now and then
by a lonely traveler.
When the song is extinguished
the wind brings words
that the trees don't understand.

Frightened leaves take refuge in the rooms.
They flee from the moss-laden tree,
that sorcerer who made a pact with night
and orders us to close the windows.

Curfew in the barracks. My friends
leave off skipping stones in the river.
For what traveler who once used to sing
do they still go on waiting in this town?

Las sombras nos tienden la mano
para llevarnos al molino
en donde junto a una muchacha
cuentan largas historias a los muros.

Rechazamos las manos de las sombras
pues sólo queremos pactar con la noche.
En un árbol hueco tumbado en el camino
se refugia un viajero,
y a ningún viajero que cantaba solitario
debe esperarse ya en este pueblo.

Poema de invierno

El invierno trae caballos blancos que resbalan en la helada.
Han encendido fuego para defender los huertos
de la bruja blanca de la helada.
Entre la blanca humareda se agita el cuidador.
El perro entumecido amenaza desde su caseta al témpano flotante de
    la luna.

    Esta noche al niño se le perdonará que duerma tarde.
    En la casa los padres están de fiesta.
    Pero él abre las ventanas
    para ver a los enmascarados jinetes
    que lo esperan en el bosque
    y sabe que su destino
    será amar el olor humilde de los senderos nocturnos.

El invierno trae aguardiente para el maquinista y el fogonero.
Una estrella perdida tambalea como baliza.
Cantos de soldados ebrios
que vuelven tarde a sus cuarteles.

En la casa ha empezado la fiesta.
Pero el niño sabe que la fiesta está en otra parte,
y mira por la ventana buscando a los desconocidos
que pasará toda la vida tratando de encontrar.

Shadows stretch out their hands to us
to take us to the mill
where next to a girl
they tell long stories to the walls.

We reject the hands of the shadows
for we wish only to make a pact with night.
In a hollow tree fallen over in the road
a traveler takes refuge,
and for no traveler who used to sing alone
should anyone be waiting in this town.

Winter Poem

Winter brings white horses that slip on the ice.
They've lit fires to defend the orchards
from the white witch of the frost.
Among clouds of white smoke, the caretaker stirs himself.
The chill-numbed dog growls from his kennel at the drifting icefloe
   of the moon.

Tonight they'll forgive the boy for sleeping late.
In the house his parents are having a party.
But he opens the windows
to see the masked horsemen
who wait for him in the forest,
and he knows his fate
will be to love the humble smell of footpaths in the night.

Winter brings moonshine for machinist and fire-stoker.
A lost star reels like a buoy.
Songs of intoxicated soldiers
returning late to their barracks.

In the house the party has begun.
But the boy knows the party's somewhere else,
and he looks through the window for the strangers
he'll spend his whole life trying to meet.

La llave

Dale la llave al otoño.
Háblale del río mudo en cuyo fondo
yace la sombra de los puentes de madera
desaparecidos hace muchos años.

No me has contado ninguno de tus secretos.
Pero tu mano es la llave que abre la puerta
del molino en ruinas donde duerme mi vida
entre polvo y más polvo,
y espectros de inviernos,
y los jinetes enlutados del viento
que huyen tras robar campanas
en las pobres aldeas.
Pero mis días serán nubes
para viajar por la primavera de tu cielo.

Saldremos en silencio.
Sin despertar al tiempo.

Te diré que podremos ser felices.

Carta de lluvia

Si atraviesas las estaciones
conservando en tus manos
la lluvia de la infancia que debimos compartir
nos reuniremos en el lugar
donde los sueños corren jubilosos
como ovejas liberadas del corral
y en donde brillará sobre nosotros
la estrella que nos fuera prometida.

> *Pero ahora te envío esta carta de lluvia*
> *que te lleva un jinete de lluvia*
> *por caminos acostumbrados a la lluvia.*

The Key

Hand over the key to autumn.
Speak to it of the mute river on whose bottom
lies the shadow of wooden bridges
vanished years ago.

You haven't told me any of your secrets.
But your hand is the key that opens the door
of the ruined mill where my life sleeps
between dust and more dust,
and ghosts of winters,
and the wind's horsemen dressed in mourning
who flee after stealing bells
in the poor villages.
But my days will be clouds
to travel through the springtime of your sky.

We'll go out in silence,
without waking up time.

I'll tell you we could be happy.

Letter of Rain

If you cross the seasons
holding in your hands
rain from the childhood we should have shared
we'll meet again in the place
where dreams run joyous
as sheep freed from the corral
and where the star we were promised
will shine over us.

> But now I send you this letter of rain
> that a horseman of rain carries to you
> over roads accustomed to the rain.

Ruega por mí, reloj,
en estas horas monótonas como ronroneos de gatos.
He vuelto al lugar que hace renacer
la ceniza de los fantasmas que odio.
Alguna vez salí al patio
a decirles a los conejos
que el amor había muerto.
Aquí no debo recordar a nadie.
Aquí debo olvidar los aromos
porque la mano que cortó aromos
ahora cava una fosa.

El pasto ha crecido demasiado.
En el techo de la casa vecina
se pudre una pelota de trapo
dejada por un niño muerto.
Entre las tablas del cerco
me vienen a mirar rostros que creía olvidados.
Mi amigo espera en vano que en el río
centellee su buena estrella.

Tú, como en mis sueños vienes
atravesando las estaciones,
con las lluvias de la infancia
en tus manos hechas cántaro.
En el invierno nos reunirá el fuego
que encenderemos juntos.
Nuestros cuerpos harán las noches tibias
como el aliento de los bueyes
y al despertar veré que el pan sobre la mesa
tiene un resplandor más grande que el de los planetas enemigos
cuando lo partan tus manos de adolescente.

> *Pero ahora te envío una carta de lluvia*
> *que te lleva un jinete de lluvia*
> *por caminos acostumbrados a la lluvia.*

Pray for me, clock,
in these hours monotonous as the purring of cats.
I've returned to the place that causes
ash of the ghosts I hate to be born again.
Once I went out to the courtyard
to tell the rabbits
that love had died.
Here I shouldn't remember anyone.
Here I should forget the myrrh trees
because the hand that cut them down
now digs a grave.

The grass has grown too high.
On the roof of the neighboring house
rots a ball of rags
left by a dead child.
Between boards of the fence
faces I thought I'd forgotten come to peer at me.
My friend waits in vain for his lucky star
to glimmer in the river.

You, as in my dreams
come crossing the seasons,
with the rain of childhood
in the pitcher of your hands.
In winter the fire we light together
will unite us.
Our bodies will make the nights warm
as the breath of oxen
and on waking I'll see the bread on the table
has a radiance greater than that of enemy planets
when your young woman's hands divide it.

> But now I send you a letter of rain
> that a horseman of rain carries to you
> over roads accustomed to the rain.

Puente en el sur

Ayer he recordado un día de claro invierno. He recordado
un puente sobre el río, un río robándole azul al cielo.
Mi amor era menos que nada en ese puente. Una naranja
hundiéndose en las aguas, una voz que no sabe a quién llama,
una gaviota cuyo brillo se deshizo entre los pinos.

Ayer he recordado que no se es nadie sobre un puente
cuando el invierno sueña con la claridad de otra estación,
y se quiere ser una hoja inmóvil en el sueño del invierno,
y el amor es menos que una naranja perdiéndose en las aguas,
menos que una gaviota cuya luz se extingue entre los pinos.

Tarjeta postal

Me decías que no me enamorara de tu hermana menor,
aquella que aún temía a los duendes
que salen de los rincones a robar nueces.
Y yo te contestaba
que en el cielo podía leer tu nombre
escrito por los pájaros
y que las nubes flotaban como los gansos
en el patio dominical de tu casa
que me hablaba con su lenguaje de gorriones.

Este domingo me veo de nuevo en el salón
mirando revistas viejas y daguerrotipos
mientras tú tocas valses en la pianola.
Alguien me ha dicho en secreto que la primavera vuelve.
La primavera vuelve pero tú no vuelves.
Tu hermana ya no cree en los duendes.
Tú no sabrías escribir mi nombre
en los vidrios cubiertos de escarcha,
y yo sólo puedo contar mis recuerdos
como un mendigo sus monedas en el frío del otoño.

Bridge in the South

Yesterday I remembered a clear winter day. I remembered
a bridge over the river, a river stealing blue from the sky.
My love was less than nothing on that bridge. An orange
sinking into the waters, a voice that doesn't know whom it calls,
a gull whose gleam was undone among the pines.

Yesterday I remembered that no one is anyone on a bridge
when winter dreams with another season's clarity,
and one wants to be a leaf motionless in the dream of winter,
and love is less than an orange losing itself in the waters,
less than a gull whose light goes out among the pines.

Postcard

You told me not to fall in love with your younger sister,
the one still afraid of elves
that come out of the corners to steal nuts.
And I answered
that in the sky I could read your name
written by birds
and that clouds floated like geese
in the Sunday courtyard of your house
that spoke to me in its language of sparrows.

This Sunday I see myself once again in the parlor
looking at old magazines and daguerrotypes
while you play waltzes on the spinet.
Someone's told me in secret that spring returns.
Spring returns but you do not.
Your sister no longer believes in elves.
You wouldn't know how to write my name
on windows covered with hoarfrost,
and all I can do is recount my memories
like a beggar his coins in the autumn cold.

Sentados frente al fuego

Sentados frente al fuego que envejece
miro su rostro sin decir palabra.
Miro el jarro de greda donde aún queda vino,
miro nuestras sombras movidas por las llamas.

Esta es la misma estación que descubrimos juntos,
a pesar de su rostro frente al fuego,
y de nuestras sombras movidas por las llamas.
Quizás si yo pudiera encontrar una palabra.

Esta es la misma estación que descubrimos juntos:
aún cae una gotera, brilla el cerezo tras la lluvia.
Pero nuestras sombras movidas por las llamas
viven más que nosotros.

Sí, ésta es la misma estación que descubrimos juntos:
—Yo llenaba esas manos de cerezas, esas
manos llenaban mi vaso de vino—.
Ella mira el fuego que envejece.

Letra de tango

La lluvia hace crecer la ciudad
como una gran rosa oxidada.
La ciudad es más grande y desierta
después que junto a las empalizadas del Barrio Estación
los padres huyen con sus hijos vestidos de marineros.
Globos sin dueños van por los tejados
y las costureras dejan de pedalear en sus máquinas.
Junto al canal que mueve sus sucias escamas
corto una brizna para un caballo escuálido
que la olfatea y después la rechaza.
Camino con el cuello del abrigo alzado
esperando ver aparecer luces de algún perdido bar

Sitting in Front of the Fire

Sitting in front of the dying fire
I look at her face without saying a word.
I look at the clay pitcher that still holds wine,
I look at our shadows stirred by the flames.

It's the same season we discovered together,
in spite of her face in front of the fire,
and our shadows stirred by the flames.
Perhaps if I could come up with a word.

It's the same season we discovered together:
the roof still leaks, the cherry tree gleams through the rain.
But our shadows stirred by the flames
are more alive than we.

Yes, it's the same season we discovered together:
—I filled those hands with cherries, those
hands filled my glass with wine.—
She looks at the dying fire.

Tango Lyric

Rain makes the city grow
like a great rusted rose.
The city is bigger and more deserted
after the fathers with their small sons dressed like sailors
flee along the stake fence of the Precinct Station.
Balloons without owners drift past the roof tiles
and seamstresses stop pedaling their machines.
Beside the canal stirring its dirty layers of scum
I break off a grass blade for a wretched horse
that sniffs and then refuses it.
I walk with the collar of my coat turned up
hoping to see the lights of some long-lost bar appear

mientras huellas de amores que nunca tuve
aparecen en mi corazón
como en la ciudad los rieles de los tranvías
que dejaron hace tanto tiempo de pasar.

Cuento de la tarde

Es tarde.
El tren del norte ha pasado.
En tu casa la cena se enfría,
las madejas ruedan
desde la falda de tu madre dormida.
He estado inmóvil mientras hablabas.
Las palabras no son nada
junto a la hoja que resucita al pasar frente a tu cara,
junto al barco de papel
que me enseñaste a hacer.
No he mirado sino tu reflejo en el estanque.

Es tarde.
Las horas son madejas rodando
desde la falda de tu madre dormida.
Volvamos al pueblo.
Las ranas repiten inútilmente su mensaje.
Te ayudo a saltar un charco, te muestro un vagabundo
encendiendo fuego en un galpón abandonado.
Estrellas irreales hacen extinguirse
las miedosas sonrisas de los tejados rojizos.
Nada debe existir.
Nada sino nuestros inmóviles reflejos
que aún retiene el estanque
y esas hojas
a veces resucitadas al pasar frente a tu cara.

while the traces of loves I never had
show up in my heart
as in the city the rails of streetcars
that so long ago stopped running.

Afternoon Story

It's late.
The train from the North has gone by.
In your house the supper gets cold,
balls of yarn roll
from your sleeping mother's lap.
I've kept still while you were talking.
Words are nothing
next to the leaf that comes to life as it passes before your face,
next to the paper boat
you taught me how to make.
I've watched nothing but your reflection in the cistern.

It's late.
The hours are balls of yarn rolling
from your sleeping mother's lap.
Let's go back to town.
The frogs repeat their message pointlessly.
I help you jump over a puddle, point out a tramp
lighting a fire in an abandoned shed.
Unreal stars make the fearful smiles
of the reddened roofs go out.
Nothing should exist.
Nothing but our motionless reflections
still held in the cistern
and those leaves
sometimes coming to life as they pass before your face.

Para hablar con los muertos

Para hablar con los muertos
hay que elegir palabras
que ellos reconozcan tan fácilmente
como sus manos
reconocían el pelaje de sus perros en la oscuridad.
Palabras claras y tranquilas
como el agua del torrente domesticada en la copa
o las sillas ordenadas por la madre
después que se han ido los invitados.
Palabras que la noche acoja
como a los fuegos fatuos los pantanos.

Para hablar con los muertos
hay que saber esperar:
ellos son miedosos
como los primeros pasos de un niño.
Pero si tenemos paciencia
un día nos responderán
con una hoja de álamo atrapado por un espejo roto,
con una llama de súbito reanimada en la chimenea,
con un regreso oscuro de pájaros
frente a la mirada de una muchacha
que aguarda inmóvil en el umbral.

Un año, otro año

*"El que durmió largo tiempo despertó en la fría tarde,
foráneo y solo en el sur donde nace la lluvia."*
                                        —Juan Cunha

I
En el confuso caserío
la luna escarcha los tejados.
El río echa espumas
de caballo enfurecido.

In Order to Talk with the Dead

In order to talk with the dead
you have to choose words
that they recognize as easily
as their hands
recognized the fur of their dogs in the dark.
Words clear and calm
as water of the torrent tamed in the wineglass
or chairs the mother puts in order
after the guests have left.
Words that night shelters
as marshes do their ghostly fires.

In order to talk with the dead
you have to know how to wait:
they are fearful
like the first steps of a child.
But if we are patient
one day they will answer us
with a poplar leaf trapped in a broken mirror,
with a flame that suddenly revives in the fireplace,
with a dark return of birds
before the glance of a girl
who waits motionless on the threshold.

One Year, Another Year

"He who slept a long time woke up in the cold afternoon,
foreign and alone in the south where the rain is born."
—Juan Cunha

I

In the hamlet's jumble of houses
the moon frosts the rooftops.
The river flings up
a raging horse's foam.

Se extingue una nube rojiza
que es el último resplandor de la fragua.

Nadie mira hacia las ventanas
despúes que el día huye
entre las humaredas de los álamos.
Ha huído este día que es siempre el mismo
como la historia contada por el anciano que perdió la memoria.

Termina el trabajo. Y todos: miedosos avaros
que alguna vez disparan contra las sombras del patio,
carpinteros ebrios, con las ropas aún llenas de virutas,
ferroviarios enhollinados, pescadores furtivos,
esperan en silencio
la hora del sueño pronunciada por relojes invisibles.

Nadie mira hacia las ventanas.
Nadie abre una puerta.
Los perros saludan a sus amos difuntos
que entran a los salones
a contemplar el retrato
que un domingo se sacaron en la plaza.
El pueblo duerme en la palma de la noche.
El pueblo se refugia en la noche
como una liebre asustada en una fosa.

II

Bebo un vaso de vino
con los amigos de todos los días.
Gruñe desganada la estufa.
El dueño del Hotel cuenta las moscas.

Los desteñidos calendarios
dicen que no se debe hablar.
"No se debe hablar", "no se debe hablar"
repiten las moscas, la estufa, la mesa
donde nos agrupamos como náufragos.
Pero bebemos mal vino
y hablamos de cosas sin asunto.

A flushed cloud is extinguished,
the last glow of the forge.

No one looks toward the windows
after the day flees
between the smoke-drifts of the poplars.
This day has fled which is always the same
like the story told by the old man who's lost his memory.

The workday ends. And everyone—fearful misers
who sometimes fire at shadows in the courtyard,
drunken carpenters with clothes still full of wood shavings,
railroad workers covered with soot, clandestine fishermen—
all wait in silence
for the hour of sleep pronounced by invisible clocks.

No one looks toward the windows.
No one opens a door.
Dogs greet their dead masters
who come into the parlors
to gaze at the portrait
taken one Sunday in the square.
The town sleeps in the palm of night.
The town takes refuge in the night
like a frightened hare in a ditch.

II
I drink a glass of wine
with my friends of every day.
The stove grumbles, reluctant.
The Hotel's owner counts the flies.

The stained calendars
say we shouldn't talk.
"We shouldn't talk," "we shouldn't talk"
repeat the flies, the stove, the table
where we huddle like the shipwrecked.
But we drink bad wine
and talk about things that don't matter.

III
El viento silba entre los alambres del telégrafo.
Malas señales: aullidos frente a una puerta que nadie abre.
Y tras la máscara del sueño
me espera el día que ahora creo abandonar.

Atardecer en automóvil

A mi hermano Iván

Abandonamos la aldea
después de beber algo en el hotel frente a la plaza.
Escogimos el camino más viejo. Pasamos lentamente
frente a tierras sin cultivar, árboles mutilados
por los roces a fuego. Entramos a una quinta abandonada
a buscar manzanas silvestres.
Luego, alguien dice: "en la estación había una muchacha
que se parecía no recuerdo a quién".
Otro empieza a cantar.
Pero cuando las estrellas salen a mirarnos
con sus húmedos ojos de ovejas tristes
nadie habla ni canta.
Trepida el viejo motor, el viento nos da en la cara,
un amigo reparte el pan y el vino. Siempre eso es bueno.
Y es bueno desear que sea eterno, eterno como creemos
son la noche, el viento, los oscuros caminos del cielo.

Cuando todos se vayan

A Eduardo Molina Ventura

Cuando todos se vayan a otros planetas
yo quedaré en la ciudad abandonada
bebiendo un último vaso de cerveza,
y luego volveré al pueblo donde siempre regreso
como el borracho a la taberna
y el niño a cabalgar
en el balancín roto.

III
Wind whistles through the telegraph wires.
Bad signs: howlings before a door no one opens.
And behind the mask of sleep
the day awaits me which now I think to abandon.

Afternoon in Automobile

For my brother Iván

We abandon the village
after a drink in the hotel facing the square.
We choose the oldest road. We drive slowly
past untilled fields, trees disfigured
by the rasp of fire. We go into an abandoned orchard
to look for wild apples.
Then someone says: "In the station there was a girl
who looked like I don't remember who."
Someone else starts to sing.
But when the stars come out to gaze at us
with their moist eyes of sad sheep
no one speaks or sings.
The old engine rattles, the wind hits us in the face,
one friend hands out the bread and wine. Always that is good.
And it's good to wish it were eternal, as we believe
in the eternity of the night, the wind, the dark roads of the sky.

When Everyone Goes Away

For Eduardo Molina Ventura

When everyone goes away to other planets
I'll stay behind in the abandoned city
drinking one last glass of beer,
then I'll go back to the town I always return to
like the drunk to the tavern
and the boy to ride horseback
on the broken seesaw.

Y en el pueblo no tendré nada que hacer,
sino echarme luciérnagas a los bolsillos
a caminar a orillas de rieles oxidados
o sentarme en el roído mostrador de un almacén
para hablar con antiguos compañeros de escuela.

Como una araña que recorre
los mismos hilos de su red
caminaré sin prisa por las calles
invadidas de malezas
mirando los palomares
que se vienen abajo,
hasta llegar a mi casa
donde me encerraré a escuchar
discos de un cantante de 1930
sin cuidarme jamás de mirar
los caminos infinitos
trazados por los cohetes en el espacio.

Fin del mundo

El día del fin del mundo
será limpio y ordenado
como el cuaderno del mejor alumno.
El borracho del pueblo
dormirá en una zanja,
el tren expreso pasará
sin detenerse en la estación,
y la banda del Regimiento
ensayará infinitamente
la marcha que toca hace veinte años en la plaza.
Sólo que algunos niños
dejarán sus volantines enredados
en los alambres telefónicos,
para volver llorando a sus casas
sin saber qué decir a sus madres
y yo grabaré mis iniciales
en la corteza de un tilo
pensando que eso no sirve para nada.

In town I'll have nothing to do
but put fireflies in my pockets
or walk along beside the rusted rails
or sit on the battered counter of a store
to talk with old pals from school.

Like a spider that goes back and forth
over the same strands of its web
I'll walk without haste through
the weed-infested streets
looking at the dovecotes
that are falling down,
until I get to my house
where I'll shut myself in to listen
to records of a singer from 1930
not bothering ever again to look
at the infinite paths
traced by rockets in outer space.

End of the World

The day the world ends
will be clean and orderly
as the best student's notebook.
The town drunk
will be asleep in a ditch,
the express train will go by
without stopping at the station,
and the Regimental band
will practice interminably
the march it's played for twenty years in the square.
Only a few children
will leave their kites tangled
in telephone wires
and go crying home
not knowing what to tell their mothers.
I'll carve my initials
in the bark of a linden tree
thinking it will do no good at all.

Los evangélicos saldrán a las esquinas
a cantar sus himnos de costumbre.
La anciana loca paseará con su quitasol.
Y yo diré: "El mundo no puede terminar
porque las palomas y los gorriones
siguen peleando por la avena en el patio."

Historia de un hijo pródigo

I

Aquí se encienden velas.
Poco a poco nos reconocen los parientes y las cosas.
La arrugada pared que recorren nuestras manos.
La escalera quejumbrosa
en donde espera un sueño
que en vano intentará cerrar nuestros ojos.

En el silencio no se sonríe a nadie.
Una niña que no sabe hablar
sigue hablando con su sombra.
La sombra de una muerta
quiere comunicarse con nosotros.

Se cierra una ventana abierta hacia el cementerio. Va a haber
   temporal.
Van a guardar los animales. Nadie se acuerda de la luna
cansada de delatar
a los ratones que roen las manzanas.
Los postes del telégrafo
hacen más vastos y desnudos los caminos.

Aquí se encienden velas.
Un espejo despierta.
En su fondo muestra la cuneta en donde mirábamos elevar
   volantines.
Una calle atravesada por un tren fatigado.
(Desde la ventanilla miramos pasar
   sin amor ni odio a nuestro pueblo.)

The evangelists will come out on the street corners
to sing their usual hymns.
The old madwoman will stroll by with her parasol.
I'll say: "The world can't end
because the pigeons and sparrows
keep on fighting over grain in the courtyard."

Story of a Prodigal Son

I
Here candles are lighted.
Little by little our parents and possessions recognize us.
The furrowed wall over which we run our hands.
The groaning staircase
where a sleep awaits
that will try in vain to close our eyes.

No one smiles at anyone in the silence.
A girl who doesn't know how to talk
goes on talking with her shadow.
The shadow of a dead woman
wants to make herself known to us.

A window open on the graveyard is closed. There's going to be a
    storm.
They're going to take in the animals. No one remembers the moon
tired of informing
on mice that gnaw the apples.
Telegraph poles
make the roads more vast and bare.

Here candles are lighted.
A mirror awakens.
Its depths reveal the drainage ditch where we used to watch kites
    rising.
A street crossed by an exhausted train.
(From the coach window with neither love
    nor hate we watch our town go by.)

Una casa donde el viento se entretiene en lanzar cartas y cuadernos
   por la ventana.
Un sendero en donde el último caballo de la tierra y una muchacha
   que aún no nace
esperan que apaguemos las velas.

> *No nos hallábamos aquí.*
> *No nos hallábamos en ninguna parte.*
> *El cuerpo de toda mujer era al fin una casa deshabitada.*
> *Las palabras de los amigos*
> *eran las mismas de los enemigos.*
> *Nuestro rostro era el rostro de un desconocido.*

Bajo las vigas soñolientas
la madre saca el pan recién nacido
del vientre tierno de la cocina.
Y el padre ofrece el vino.

II

Porque una niña que no sabe hablar habla con su sombra.
Porque esta noche deben encenderse velas,
y un espejo y un temporal cuentan nuestra historia.
Porque una ventana se ha cerrado tras la última mirada al
   cementerio del cerro.
Porque nos han ofrecido el pan y el vino,
así como toda la vía láctea cabe en el cuadrado de la ventana,
cabe en un solo momento de esta herrumbrosa noche
el tiempo verdadero del cual nos vienen las semillas del pan y el
   vino.
El tiempo donde todos bebíamos al final de la jornada
rodeados de la música de las constelaciones y los árboles,
mientras las mujeres esperaban en el hogar, junto a niños y frutos
   dormidos.

III

La madre apaga el fuego de la cocina y lleva a la niña a su lecho.
El temporal habla a la casa en el lenguaje que olvidamos.
El padre nos acoge, pero no lo reconocemos.

A house where the wind amuses itself throwing letters
   and notebooks out the window.
A path where the last horse on earth and a girl who's not yet born
wait for us to blow out the candles.

We didn't find ourselves here.
We didn't find ourselves anywhere.
In the end, every woman's body was a deserted house.
The words of friends
were the same as those of enemies.
Our face was the face of a stranger.

Under the sleepy roofbeams
the mother removes the newborn bread
from the soft womb of the kitchen.
And the father offers wine.

II

Because a girl who doesn't know how to talk
   talks with her shadow.
Because candles should be lit tonight,
and a mirror and a rainstorm tell our story.
Because a window's been closed after a last look at the graveyard on
   the hill.
Because they've offered us the bread and wine,
just as the entire Milky Way fits into the frame of the window,
so the true time when the seeds of the bread and wine come to us
fits into a single moment of this rusted night.
The time we all used to drink at the workday's end
surrounded by the music of constellations and trees,
while the women waited at home, with sleeping children and
   crops.

III

The mother puts out the kitchen fire and carries her daughter
   to bed.
The storm speaks to the house in a language we've forgotten.
Our father receives us, but we don't acknowledge him.

Quizás nuestros rostros queden en el espejo, junto al último caballo
de la tierra, y una muchacha que no ha nacido.
Hemos consumido el fuego y el vino.
Los caminos que van a la Ciudad nos esperan.

Otro cantar

Mientras el resplandor del mediodía
Torna más oscuros a los hombres en sus fosas
Las semillas del sol
Hallado en los bolsillos de mi vieja camisa
Hacen germinar todas mis horas

Despójenme de cuanto tengo
Un pájaro volando vale más que cien en la mano
Con mi alfabeto dispongo de lo que necesito
Abejas bosques cardos arroyuelos
Y un vaso de vino canta
La canción de la sola golondrina
Que hace para mí el verano
La canción de todos los blancos ramos
De un porvenir que aún guarda silencio

Señales

Atardece. Se disuelven
las lejanas humaredas de los cerros.
Los gorriones picotean cerezas pasadas.
El tren de carga pasa
dejando una estela de carbón y mugidos.

"Si llueve con creciente va a llover siete días."
Los rieles se alargan sin esperanza
mientras el tiempo se despoja de su máscara
y muestra su rostro secreto en la lluvia.

En la trastienda del almacén
alzan sus vasos de pipeño los amigos. En la plazuela

Maybe our faces remain in the mirror, next to the last horse on
    earth, and a girl who's not been born.
We've consumed the fire and the wine.
The roads that lead to the City await us.

Another Song

While the midday brilliance
Turns men darker in their graves
The seeds from the sun
I found in the pockets of my old shirt
Make all my hours flourish

Strip me of everything I have
A bird in the bush is worth a hundred in the hand
With the alphabet I have all I need at my disposal
Bees forests thistles creekbeds
And a glass of wine sings
The song of the one swallow
That makes for me the summer
The song of all the white branches
Of a future that still keeps silent

Signs

Night falls. The hills'
distant clouds of mist dissolve.
Sparrows peck the spoiled cherries.
The freight train goes by
leaving a wake of coal-smoke and lowings.

"If it rains at the crescent it'll rain seven days."
The rails stretch hopelessly away
as time tears off its mask
and shows its secret face in the rain.

In the back room of the store
friends raise their glasses of new wine. In the little square

el forastero oye contar estrellas a los hijos del carpintero.
Y luego una ronda: "Alicia va en el coche, carolín . . ."

El pueblo se refugia en los ojos de ovejas que dormitan.
Antes de irse, el sol ilumina brutalmente
nuestro rostro condenado al fracaso.
Nuestro rostro
y los de quienes nunca conocerán la realidad,
dispersándose como el polvillo de los duraznos en los dedos del
    viento. Jinetes perdidos, novias
que aún esperan en la capilla ruinosa, vagabundos
con la cabeza destrozada por las locomotoras.

El sueño hace señas con su linterna oxidada.
El Angel de la Guarda ya no espera nuestro ruego.
Y vemos sin temor que se abre para nosotros
el país de la noche sin fronteras.

Los Conjuros

A Enrique Rebolledo

Los temerosos de los brujos vecinos
lanzan puñados de sal al fuego
cuando pasan las aves agoreras.
Los buscadores de entierros
en sueños hallan monedas de oro.
Los despierta el jinete del rayo
cayendo hecho llamas entre ellos.

Medianoche de San Juan. Las higueras
se visten para la fiesta.
Eco de gemidos de animales
hundidos hace milenios en los pantanos.
Los chimalenes reúnen las ovejas
que huyen del corral.
Aúllan los perros en casa del avaro
que quiere pactar con el Malo.

the one who's come home a stranger hears the carpenter's children
    counting stars.
And then a round: "Alicia rides in the carriage, Carolín . . ."

The town takes refuge in the drowsy eyes of sheep.
Before it goes, the sun brutally lights up
our face condemned to failure.
Our face, and the faces
of those who'll never know what's real,
scattering like dust from peach trees in fingers of the wind. Lost
    horsemen, brides
who still wait in the ruined chapel, tramps
with heads shattered by locomotives.

Sleep signals with its rusted lantern.
The Angel of the Guard no longer awaits our plea.
And we see without fear that the land
of unbordered night opens for us.

The Exorcisms

For Enrique Rebolledo

Those afraid of the sorcerers next door
throw fistfuls of salt in the fire
when the birds of ill omen fly over.
Those hunting for buried treasure
find gold coins in their dreams.
They are awakened by the horseman of the thunderbolt
falling in flames among them.

Midsummer midnight. The fig trees
dress up for the feast.
Echo of groanings of animals
submerged for millennia in the swamps.
Indian herders round up the sheep
that flee the corral.
Dogs howl in the house of the miser
who wants to make a pact with the Evil One.

Ya no reconozco mi casa.
En ella caen luces de estrellas en ruinas.
Mi amiga vela frente a un espejo:
espera allí aparezca el desconocido
anunciado por las sombras más largas del año.

Al alba, anidan lechuzas en las higueras.
En los rescoldos amanecen huellas de manos de brujos.
Despierto teniendo en mis manos hierbas y tierra
de un lugar donde nunca estuve.

Linterna sorda

Un hombre verá cosas invisibles.
Cuando los deudos lo abandonen
y las canoas vengan desde el oeste,
cuando los deudos a escondidas hayan dejado los panes redondos y
    sacrificado los caballos,
las hijas del guardahilos tendrán miedo
de ver pasar su ánima al atardecer
y los forasteros tendrán visiones que los harán gemir en sueños.

Un hombre, entonces, se desprende del sol y de la luna.

Molino de madera

Era un puerto donde desembocaba el trigo.
Terminaba su viaje en el molino
la espiga, transformada en bella harina.

Había una bodega enorme, donde los fuertes sacos
plenos de maduros cereales
pugnaban por trepar hasta las vigas.

En el verano el sol iluminaba los patios,
la madera nueva.
Los portones se abrían y entraban las carretas.

I no longer recognize my house.
Into it falls the light of ruined stars.
My friend keeps watch before the mirror:
she hopes the stranger shows up there
announced by the longest shadows of the year.

At dawn, barn owls nest in the fig trees.
In the glowing coals appear the handprints of sorcerers.
I awaken, holding in my hands herbs and earth
from a place I never was.

Dark Lantern

A man will see invisible things.
When his kinfolk abandon him
and the canoes come from the west,
when his kinfolk have left the round loaves on the sly and
    sacrificed the horses,
the yarnkeeper's daughters will dread
seeing his spirit go by in the late afternoon,
and those who come home as strangers will have visions that make
    them whimper in their dreams.

A man, then, emerges from the sun and the moon.

Wooden Mill

It was a port the wheat flowed into.
The tassels ended their journey
in the mill, transformed to lovely flour.

There was an immense warehouse, where sturdy sacks
stuffed with ripe grain
struggled to mount to the beams.

In summer, sun lit up the courtyards,
the new wood.
The big gates opened and the carts came in.

El molinero tenía hasta las pestañas blancas
y su cantar aceitaba las máquinas.

Ahora, el cielo se pone más gris cuando lo mira.
Desde una ventana hecha pedazos
se ve correr a sus pies
al río vencedor, retumbando, royendo los cimientos.
La gente lo rehuye. Quizás albergue al Diablo.

Y entre la humedad y el moho,
abriendo puertas oxidadas, riendo ante las máquinas,
se pasean los duendes blancos
nacidos de la antigua harina.

La tierra de la noche

No hablemos.
Es mejor abrir las ventanas mudas
desde la muerte de la hermana mayor.
La voz de la hierba hace callar la noche:
Hace un mes no llueve.
Nidos vacíos caen desde la enredadera.
Los cerezos se apagan como añejas canciones.
Este mes será de los muertos.
Este mes será del espectro
de la luna de verano.

Sigue brillando, luna de verano.
Reviven los escalones de piedra
gastados por los pasos de los antepasados.
Los murciélagos no dejan de chillar
entre los muros ruinosos de la Cervecería.
El azadón roto
espera tierra fresca de nuevas tumbas.
Y nosotros no debemos hablar
cuando la luna brilla
más blanca y despiadada que los huesos de los muertos.

Sigue brillando, luna de verano.

Even the miller's eyelashes were white
and his singing oiled the machines.

Now when it looks at the mill, the sky grows grayer.
From a shattered window
the victorious river can be seen
running at the mill's feet, thundering, gnawing the foundations.
People leave it alone. Maybe it houses the Devil.

Among the dampness and mold,
opening rusted doors, laughing before the machines,
the white elves stroll,
born of the ancient wheat.

The Land of Night

Let's not talk.
It's better to open the windows, mute
since the eldest sister's death.
The voice of the grass makes the night fall silent:
No rain for a month.
Empty nests fall from the climbing vine.
The cherry trees are extinguished like stale songs.
This month will be for the dead.
This month will be for the spectre
of the summer moon.

Keep on shining, summer moon.
The stone stairs worn
by the footsteps of ancestors revive.
Bats don't cease shrilling
between the ruined walls of the Brewery.
The broken hoe
awaits fresh earth of new tombs.
And we shouldn't talk
when the moon shines
whiter and more pitiless than the bones of the dead.

Keep on shining, summer moon.

En memoria de una casa cerrada

Mi amigo se atreve a tocar la guitarra
que en herencia le dejó su padre.
Los pasos del muerto resuenan
por las galerías desiertas.
Una sombra se sienta
frente a la chimenea apagada.

En la cocina quedaron
tazas rotas, ollas sucias.
Junto al cerco,
bajo una desordenada llovizna,
el silencio recién llegado
se hace amigo de los perros.

Frente a la puerta cerrada
nos estrechamos las manos
y partimos sin mirar atrás.

Juegos

A Sebastián y Carolina

Los niños juegan en sillas diminutas,
los grandes no tienen nada con que jugar.
Los grandes dicen a los niños
que se debe hablar en voz baja.
Los grandes están de pie
junto a la luz ruinosa de la tarde.

Los niños reciben de la noche
los cuentos que llegan
como un tropel de terneros manchados,
mientras los grandes repiten
que se deben hablar en voz baja.

In Memory of a Closed House

My friend dares to play the guitar
that his father left to him.
The footsteps of the dead man echo
through the deserted corridors.
A shadow sits down
before the fireplace gone out.

In the kitchen, broken cups,
dirty cooking pots remain.
Next to the fence,
under a sloppy drizzle,
the newly arrived silence
makes friends with the dogs.

Before the closed door
we shake hands
and part without looking back.

Games

For Sebastián and Carolina

The children play in tiny chairs,
the grownups have nothing to play with.
The grownups tell the children
they should keep their voices down.
The grownups are standing
by the ruinous light of afternoon.

The children receive from the night
stories that arrive
like a stampede of speckled calves,
while the grownups repeat
that they should keep their voices down.

Los niños se esconden
bajo la escalera de caracol
contando sus historias incontables
como mazorcas asoleándose en los techos
y para los grandes sólo llega el silencio
vacío como un muro que ya no recorren sombras.

Imagen

Te reconoces
en ese niño que esta mañana de escarcha
sale a comprar pan
y saluda al lechero
cuyo silbato despierta las calles.

Tú eres ese niño
y eres el niño que a campo traviesa
va hacia la casa de los vecinos
con un ganso bajo el brazo
bajo la luna espiada por cohetes
en la que no se verán nunca más
la Virgen, San José y el Niño.

A un niño en un árbol

Eres el único habitante
de una isla que sólo tú conoces,
rodeada del oleaje del viento
y del silencio rozado apenas
por las alas de una lechuza.

Ves un arado roto
y una trilladora cuyo esqueleto
permite un último relumbre del sol.
Ves al verano convertido en un espantapájaros
cuyas pesadillas angustian los sembrados.
Ves la acequia en cuyo fondo tu amigo desaparecido
toma el barco de papel que echaste a navegar.

The children hide
under the spiral staircase
recounting their stories, countless
as ears of corn drying in the sun on rooftops,
and for the grownups only silence arrives,
empty as a wall the shadows no longer pass over.

Image

You recognize yourself
in that child who goes out to buy bread
this morning of frost
and greets the milkman
whose whistle wakes up the streets.

You are that child
and the child who cuts across the field
to the neighbors' house
with a goose under his arm
under a moon monitored by rockets
in which no one will ever see again
the Virgin, Saint Joseph, and the Child.

To a Child in a Tree

You're the sole inhabitant
of an island only you know about,
surrounded by surging waves of wind
and silence barely grazed
by the barn owl's wings.

You see a broken plough
and a thresher whose skeleton
lets pass a final gleam of sun.
You see summer turned into a scarecrow
whose nightmares torment the cropland.
You see the irrigation ditch in whose depths your vanished friend
takes hold of the paper ship you set afloat.

Ves al pueblo y los campos extendidos
como las páginas del silabario
donde un día sabrás que leíste
la historia de la felicidad.

El almacenero sale a cerrar los postigos.
Las hijas del granjero encierran las gallinas.
Ojos de extraños peces
miran amenazantes desde el cielo.
Hay que volver a tierra.
Tu perro viene a saltos a encontrarte.
Tu isla se hunde en el mar de la noche.

Frutos del verano

I
La sombra de una hoja
Es el recuerdo de nuestro futuro
Pasan niños ciegos
Ellos siempre tendrán hambre del sol
Demos vuelta la hoja de este día

II
No desdeño la realidad
La realidad un puñado de arena una pesadilla
Los puentes se curvan
Bajo el paso de regimientos que cantan
Historias de manzanos florecidos
Y las canoas se abren como vainas de arvejas

III
Querríamos cambiar lámparas nuevas por viejas
Escogimos guijarros redondos
En vez de pronunciar una palabra
Se regresa de países que no se pueden ver

IV
Tal vez es triste haberse amado
Haberse amado haberle puesto nombre a un árbol

You see the town and the fields spread out
like the pages of the primer
where one day you'll know you've read
the history of joy.

The storekeeper comes out to close the shutters.
The farmer's daughters shoo in the chickens.
Eyes of strange fish
look down menacingly from the sky.
It's time to come back to earth.
Your dog bounds up to meet you.
Your island sinks into the sea of night.

Fruits of Summer

I
The shadow of a leaf
Is the memory of our future
Blind children go by
They'll always be hungry for the sun
Let's turn the page of this day

II
I don't disdain reality
Reality a fistful of sand a nightmare
The bridges bend
Under the step of singing regiments
Tales of apple trees in flower
And the canoes open like green pea pods

III
We'd like to change new lamps for old
We select round pebbles
Instead of uttering a word
One returns from countries that cannot be seen

IV
Perhaps it's sad to have loved each other
To have loved to have given a name to a tree

Una mano se vuelve pájaro sin jaula
Sol que los primeros hombres temen no volver a ver
Y aún no se ha descubierto el fuego.

Edad de oro

Un día u otro
todos seremos felices.
Yo estaré libre
de mi sombra y mi nombre.
El que tuvo temor
escuchará junto a los suyos
los pasos de su madre,
el rostro de la amada será siempre joven
al reflejo de la luz antigua en la ventana,
y el padre hallará en la despensa la linterna
para buscar en el patio
la navaja extraviada.

No sabremos
si la caja de música
suena durante horas o un minuto;
tú hallarás—sin sorpresa—
el atlas sobre el cual soñaste con extraños países,
tendrás en tus manos
un pez venido del río de tu pueblo,
y Ella alzará sus párpados
y será de nuevo pura y grave
como las piedras lavadas por la lluvia.

Todos nos reuniremos
bajo la solemne y aburrida mirada
de personas que nunca han existido,
y nos saludaremos sonriendo apenas
pues todavía creeremos estar vivos.

A hand turns into a bird without a cage
Sun that the first men fear they'll never see again
And fire hasn't even been discovered.

Golden Age

One of these days
we'll all be happy.
I'll be free
of my shadow and my name.
He who was afraid
will hear his mother's footsteps
next to his own,
the beloved's face will always be young
in the antique lamp's reflection in the window,
the father will find a lantern in the pantry
to search in the courtyard
for the misplaced razor.

We won't know
if the music box
plays for hours or a minute;
you'll find—without surprise—
the atlas over which you dreamed about strange lands,
you'll hold in your hands
a fish from the river of your town,
and She will raise her eyelids
and once again be pure and serious
as stones washed by the rain.

We'll all meet
under the solemn, bored gaze
of people who've never existed,
and we'll greet each other almost smiling
for we'll still believe we're alive.

Los trenes de la noche

1

El puente en medio de la noche
blanquea como la osamenta de un buey.
Entre la niebla desgarrada de los sauces
debían aparecer fantasmas,
pero sólo pudimos ver
el fugaz reflejo de los vagones en el río
y las luces harapientas
de las chozas de los areneros.

2

Nos alejamos de la ciudad
balanceándonos junto al viento
en la plataforma del último carro
del tren nocturno.

Pronto amanecerá.
Los fríos gritos de los queltehues
despiertan a los pueblos
donde sólo brilla la luz
de un prostíbulo de cara trasnochada.

Pronto amanecerá.
En las ciudades
miles de manos se alargan
para acallar furiosos despertadores.

Pronto amanecerá.
Las estrellas desaparecen

Los trenes de la noche
(Night Trains)
(1964, 1971)

Night Trains

1
The bridge in the middle of the night
whitens like an ox's skeleton.
Among the clawed mist of willows
spirits should have appeared,
but we could see only
the fleeting reflections of boxcars in the river
and ragged lights
from the sand peddlers' shanties.

2
We pull away from the city
rocking next to the wind
on the platform of the night train's
final car.

Soon it will be dawn.
The *queltehue* birds' cold cries
wake up the towns
where light shines only
from a brothel with an all-night face.

Soon it will be dawn.
In the cities
thousands of hands reach out
to silence alarm clocks going like mad.

Soon it will be dawn.
The stars vanish

como semillas de girasol
en el buche de los gorriones.
Los tejados palpitan en carne viva
bajo las manos de la mañana.

Y el viento que nos siguió toda la noche
con cantos aprendidos
de torrentes donde no llega el sol,
ahora es ese niño desconocido
que se despierta para saludarnos
desde un cerezo resucitado.

3

Recuerdo la Estación Central
en el atardecer de un día de diciembre.
Me veo apenas con dinero para tomar una cerveza,
despeinado, sediento, inmóvil,
mientras parte el tren en donde viaja una muchacha
que se ha ido diciendo que nunca me querrá,
que se acostaría con cualquiera, menos conmigo,
que ni siquiera me escribirá una carta.
Es en la Estación Central
un sofocante atardecer
de un día de diciembre.

4

En la estación de Renaico
un caballo blanco enganchado a un coche
espera sin impacientarse.
Espera bajo toda la lluvia
destilada por el mantel sucio del cielo,
rodeado de toda la soledad
de un mundo redondo e infinito.

5

Los pinos descortezados y nudosos
pasan interminablemente delante de nosotros,
y nos miran hasta que nos damos cuenta
de que su rostro es el rostro
de nuestros verdaderos antepasados.

like sunflower seeds
in the crops of sparrows.
Rooftops throb stark naked
under the hands of morning.

And the wind that followed us all night
with songs learned
from torrents the sun never reaches,
is now that unknown child
who wakes up to wave to us
from the resurrected cherry tree.

3

I remember the Central Station
in the late afternoon of a December day.
There I am with hardly enough money for a beer,
inert, thirsty, my hair a mess,
while the train departs with a girl
who's gone off saying she'll never love me,
who'd go to bed with anyone but me,
who won't even write me a letter.
It's a stifling afternoon
in the Central Station
on a December day.

4

In the Renaico station
a white horse hitched to a carriage
waits without impatience.
Waits under all the rain
filtered through the dirty tablecloth of the sky,
surrounded by all the solitude
of a round and infinite world.

5

The bark-stripped, knotty pines
pass endlessly before us,
and they look at us until we realize
that their face is the face
of our true ancestors.

6

Cuando el pequeño tren se anima a subir la cuesta
mira temeroso a la luna
que lo contempla con la misma cara airada
con que el reloj de cocina mira al adolescente
que por primera vez llega tarde a casa.

7

El sol apenas tuvo tiempo para despedirse
escribiendo largas frases
con la negra y taciturna sombra
de los vagones de carga abandonados.
Y en la profunda tarde sólo se oye
el lamentable susurro
de los cardos resecos.

8

Una estrella nueva
sobre los cercos rotos.
Sobre los cercos rotos de orillas de la línea
a los que vienen a robar tablas este invierno
los habitantes de las poblaciones callampas.

9

Yo hubiese querido ver de nuevo
el pañuelo de campesina pobre
con que amarraste tu cabellera desordenada por el puelche,
tus mejillas partidas por la escarcha
de las duras mañanas del sur,
tu gesto de despedida
en el andén de la pequeña estación,
para no soñar siempre contigo
cuando en la noche de los trenes
mi cara se vuelve hacia esa aldea
que ahogaron las poderosas aguas.

10

Qué hacer en este cuarto de hotel de provincia
después de viajar todo el santo día,

6

When the little train summons its forces to climb the hill
it looks fearfully at the moon
that regards it with the same irritated face
as the kitchen clock watching the teenager
the first time he comes home late.

7

The sun hardly had time to say goodbye
writing long sentences
with the black and taciturn shadow
of abandoned freight cars.
And deep into the afternoon all you can hear
is the pitiful rustle
of desiccated thistles.

8

A new star
over broken fences.
Over broken fences at the edges of the track
where the shantytown dwellers
come to steal boards this winter.

9

I had hoped to see once more
the poor peasant woman's kerchief
with which you tied back your hair blown about by the *puelche*
    wind,
your cheeks cracked by the frost
of hard mornings in the south,
your farewell gesture
on the platform of the tiny station,
so as not always to dream of you
when in the train-filled night
my face turns toward that village
drowned by the mighty waters.

10

What to do in that provincial hotel room
after traveling the whole blessed day,

sino tenderse en la sucia cama
a hojear revistas de hace treinta años
donde sonríe Al Jolson y aún vuelan dirigibles,
sin poder dejar de oír los oscuros silbatos
que vienen de los patios ferroviarios.

11

Con un amigo espero la pasada
del Expreso de las 23,15—
ese tren fugaz como botella de vino
en manos de mi amigo y yo.
Tendidos bajo las estrellas tiernas
como los agujeros en la carpa de un circo pobre
mi amigo habla de una muchacha
a la que espera ver a la pasada del Expreso.

Yo no espero ver
sino esas sombras que recorren los cercos en busca de mi sombra.
No espero escuchar sino esos pasos
que vienen desde el aserradero incendiado.
No espero ver sino los pedazos de botella
que la luna hace brillar entre los rieles,
y no espero oír
sino los maullidos del gato perdido entre los geranios
que cuidó la hija enferma del guardacruzadas.

El oleaje del Expreso
pasa remeciendo la Estación.
Mientras mi amigo corre
hacia ventanas iluminadas y sin rostros,
yo escondo tras los dedos del pasto
mi cara resquebrajada como una hoja
cansada de soportar el peso de la noche.

12

El silbato del conductor
es un guijarro
cayendo al pozo gris de la tarde.

but stretch out on the grubby bed
to leaf through magazines of thirty years ago
where Al Jolson grins and dirigibles still fly,
and it's impossible not to hear the muffled
whistles from the railroad yards.

11
I wait with a friend
for the 11:15 Express to go by—
that train fleeting as a bottle of wine
in the hands of my friend and me.
Stretched out under stars tender
as holes in the tent of a pauper circus,
my friend talks about a girl
he expects to see as the Express goes by.

I expect to see nothing
but those shadows that prowl along the fences in search of my
    shadow.
I expect to listen to nothing but those footsteps
that come from the burned-down sawmill.
I expect to see nothing but bottle shards
the moon makes gleam between the rails,
and I expect to hear nothing
but the yowls of a cat lost among geraniums
that the flagman's sick daughter once tended.

The Express goes by,
rocking the station in its wake.
While my friend runs
toward lighted faceless windows,
I hide behind fingers of grass,
my face split like a leaf
weary of holding up the weight of night.

12
The conductor's whistle
is a pebble
falling into the gray well of afternoon.

El tren parte con resoplidos
de boxeador fatigado.
El tren parte en dos al pueblo
como cuchillo que rebana pan caliente.
Los vagabundos quedan mirando
a los niños que corren entre castillos de madera.
De las chozas dispersas a lo largo de la vía
salen mujeres a recoger carboncillo entre los rieles,
otras reúnen la parchada ropa
crucificada en los alambres
tendidos en los patios llenos de humo,
y algunas inmóviles y serias como grandes sandías
recogen en los umbrales el lerdo sol de fines de otoño.

13

Sobre el techo recién pintado de azarcón
de la bodega triguera
enredada en la humareda que deja el tren nocturno
aparece una luna con cara de campesino borracho,
enrojecida por el resplandor de los roces a fuego.

14

Podremos saber
que nada vale más
que la brizna roída por un conejo
o la ortiga creciendo
entre las grietas de los muros.
Pero nunca dejaremos de correr
para acompañar a los niños
a saludar el paso de los trenes.

15

Los pueblos se arremolinan en mi memoria
como páginas de un libro arrancadas por una ventolera:
Renaico, Lolenco, Mininco, Las Viñas,
Púa, Perquenco, Quillén y Lautaro.

De nuevo aparecen con sus postes de telégrafo
derribados por el último temporal,
con sus casas afirmadas hombro a hombro

The train departs, panting
like an exhausted boxer.
The train parts the town in two
like a knife slicing warm bread.
Tramps linger, watching children
who run between castles made of wood.
From shanties scattered along the track
come women to collect coal chips between the rails,
others gather patched clothing
crucified on wires
strung in the smoke-filled yards,
and some, inert and serious as immense watermelons,
collect in doorways the dull-witted sun of autumn's end.

13

Above the freshly painted metal roof
of the wheat silo,
wrapped in the plume of smoke the night train leaves behind,
appears a moon with the face of a drunken peasant,
reddened by the glow of burning stubble.

14

We may know
that nothing is worth more
than grass gnawed by a rabbit
or nettles growing
in fissures in the wall.
But we'll never stop running,
going with the children
to wave to passing trains.

15

Towns get mixed up in my memory
like pages of a book yanked out by a wind-blast:
Renaico, Lolenco, Mininco, Las Viñas,
Púa, Perquenco, Quillén, and Lautaro.

They appear once again with their telegraph poles
knocked down in the last rainstorm,
with their houses steadying themselves shoulder-to-shoulder

como ancianas que se emborrachan
para recordar las fiestas de principios de siglo.

Los pueblos flotan en mi cabeza
que he inundado de vino en este largo viaje
como flotan los viejos troncos
en los ríos en crecida.

Inundo de vino mi cabeza
para olvidar la cancioncilla senil
que tararea el carro de tercera,
para olvidar a los torpes campesinos
con sus canastos con quesos o gallinas,
y a los viajantes que ofrecen naipes y peinetas.

Cierro los ojos
y afirmo mi frente enhollinada
en los vidrios de la ventanilla
mientras la noche hunde en los ríos
su frente arrugada por los peces.

16

Ha terminado el verano.
Regreso al pueblo como tantas otras veces
en el sudoroso tren de la tarde.
Ha terminado el verano,
no sin antes marchitar los girasoles,
no sin antes resecar los cardos que crecen junto a los rieles.
A la ciudad debía acompañarme el viento del sur.
El viento que se queda rondando por los campos y es el sereno
que los villorrios escuchan todo el invierno
como serenos que en caserones ruinosos pegan sus oídos a relojes
    sin agujas.
El viento que barre con cardos y girasoles.
El viento que siempre tiene la razón y todo lo torna vacío.
El viento.

Quizás debiera quedarme en este pueblo
como en una tediosa sala de espera.

like old women getting drunk
to recall parties from the turn of the century.

The towns drift in my head,
which I've flooded with wine on this long trip,
the way ancient tree trunks drift
on the rising rivers.

I flood my head with wine
to forget the senile little tune
the third-class car is humming,
to forget the clumsy peasants
with their baskets of cheese or chickens,
and traveling salesmen who offer playing cards and combs.

I close my eyes
and rest my sooty forehead
on the window glass
while night plunges its fish-wrinkled
brow into the rivers.

16

Summer is over.
I go back to town as I have so many times
in the sweaty afternoon train.
Summer is over,
not without first withering the sunflowers,
not without drying up the thistles that grow beside the rails.
The south wind should come with me to the city.
The wind that goes on patrolling the fields and is the night
 watchman
the little hick towns listen to all winter
like night watchmen in tumble-down mansions who press their
 ears to clocks without hands.
The wind that sweeps up with thistles and sunflowers.
The wind that's always in the right and empties everything.
The wind.

Maybe I should stay in this town
as in a tedious waiting room.

En este pueblo o en cualquier pueblo
de esos cuyos nombres ya no se pueden leer en el retorcido letrero
   indicador.
Quedarme
escribiendo largos poemas deshilvanados
en el reverso de calendarios inservibles
sin preocuparme de que nadie los lea o no los lea,
o conversando con amigos aburridores
sobre política, fútbol o viajes por el espacio
mientras tictaquean las goteras del bar.

Todo empieza a quedar en penumbras.
El viento apaga la luz de los últimos girasoles.
Todo está en penumbras.
La campana anuncia la llegada del tren
y siento el mismo temor del alumno nuevo
cuando sus compañeros lo rodean
en el patio de cemento de la escuela.

Pero debo dejar el pueblo
como quien lanza una colilla al suelo:
después de todo, ya se sabe bien
que en cualquier parte *la vida es demasiado cotidiana.* *

Hasta luego: rieles, girasoles,
maderas dormidas en los carros planos,
caballos apaleados por los carretoneros,
carretilla mohosa en el patio de la casa del jefe-estación.

Hasta luego,
hasta luego.
Hasta que nos encontremos sin sorpresa
viajando por los trenes de la noche
bajo unos párpados cerrados.

   Santiago-Lautaro, 1963

*Jules Laforgue

In this town or any other
of those towns whose names you can no longer read on the twisted
    direction sign.
To stay
writing long, disjointed poems
on the backs of obsolete calendars,
not caring if anyone reads them or not,
or chatting with tiresome friends
about politics, soccer, or trips through space
while leaks drip onto the bar.

Everything starts to move into shadow.
The wind puts out the light of the last sunflowers.
Everything's in shadow.
The bell announces the train's arrival
and I feel the same terror as the new student
when his classmates surround him
on the cement playground of the school.

But I should leave town
like one who throws a cigarette butt to the ground:
after all, it's well known
that anywhere *life is too mundane.**

Farewell: rails, sunflowers,
lumber drowsing on the flatcars,
horses flogged by the draymen,
moldy wheelbarrow in the yard of the stationmaster's house.

Farewell,
farewell.
Until we meet each other not surprised
traveling on the night trains
under closed eyelids.

   Santiago-Lautaro, 1963

*Jules Laforgue

PART TWO

Poems from *Para un pueblo fantasma*
(For a Town of Ghosts)
(1978)

Nadie ha muerto aún en esta casa

Nadie ha muerto aún en esta casa.
Los presagios del nogal
aún no se descifran
y los pasos que regresan
siempre son los conocidos.

Nadie ha muerto aún en esta casa.
Lo piensan las pesadas cabezas de las rosas
donde el ocioso rocío se columpia
mientras el gusano se enrosca amenazante
en las estériles garras de las viñas.

Nadie ha muerto aún en esta casa.
Ninguna mano busca una mano ausente.
El fuego aún no añora a quien cuidó encenderlo.
La noche no ha cobrado sus poderes.

Nadie ha muerto pero todos han muerto.
Rostros desconocidos se asoman a los espejos
otros conducen hacia otros pueblos nuestros coches.
Yo miro un huerto cuyos frutos recuerdo.

Sólo se oyen los pasos habituales.
El fuego enseña a los niños su lenguaje
el rocío se divierte columpiándose en las rosas.
Nadie ha muerto aún en esta casa.

From *Nadie ha muerto aún en esta casa*
(Nobody's Died Yet in This House)
(1978)

Nobody's Died Yet in This House

Nobody's died yet in this house.
The walnut tree's omens
are not yet deciphered
and returning footsteps
are always the ones we know.

Nobody's died yet in this house.
That's what the heavy heads of roses think,
where the do-nothing dew swings
while the worm twists menacingly
in the vineyards' sterile talons.

Nobody's died yet in this house.
No hand seeks an absent hand.
The fire doesn't yet yearn for the one who took care to light it.
Night hasn't collected its powers.

Nobody's died but everybody has.
Unknown faces show up in the mirrors,
others drive our cars to other towns.
I look at an orchard whose fruits I remember.

Only the usual footsteps are heard.
Fire teaches the children its tongue,
dew amuses itself swinging in the roses.
Nobody's died yet in this house.

Aperitivo

En el Bar del Hotel de France
Pierdo el tiempo para ganar la esperanza
El corazón parpadea como una hoja
Junto al parpadear de cien hojas verdes
De las muchachas que te olvidaron
Tú podrías recobrar a una
Que era una manzana silvestre
Apenas tocada por la primera helada
Pero el aperitivo es tierno
Como un jilguero sobre un alambre de púa
Como el olor de la tierra tras el riego
Como la cansada luz de una bicicleta
En el camino donde el cartero se ha perdido
Ebrio como yo a mediodía.

Siete para un secreto

"Dad de beber al cuervo
que dio de beber a los marinos".
Así oí cantar el Día de San Valentín
a una niña que mendigaba a fines del Siglo XVIII
bajo la muestra de una posada de Bristol.

Siete cuervos saben el secreto:
uno está en la Calle de la Vieja Linterna,
otro bate sus alas sobre el amigo que será enterrado frente a un
    muro,
otro sigue diciendo "Nevermore",
otro cuida que el hijo del molinero no reciba más trigo,
otro es dueño del letrero que en una estación
indicaba el nombre de no se sabe ya qué pueblo,
otro vigila tres lirios que en vano esperan un jinete,
pero el último me dice que volveré a estar dentro de una canción
    de otro siglo
y regresaré a entregar la moneda que le debo a una muchacha.

Aperitif

In the bar of the Hotel de France
I waste time getting my hopes up
My heart flutters like a leaf
Beside the fluttering of a hundred green leaves
Of the girls who forgot you
You could recover one of them
Who was a wild apple
Hardly touched by the first frost
But the aperitif is delicate
Like a linnet on a strand of barbed wire
Like the smell of the earth after watering
Like the tired light of a bicycle
On the road where the postman has lost his way
Tipsy like me in the middle of the day.

Seven for a Secret

"Give the crow to drink
what it gave to the sailors."
So I heard them sing on Saint Valentine's Day
to a girl who was begging at the end of the 18th Century
under the sign of a Bristol inn.

Seven crows know the secret:
one is in Old Lantern Street,
another beats its wings over the friend who'll be buried in front of
   a wall,
another goes on saying "Nevermore,"
another makes sure the miller's son gets no more wheat,
another is owner of the signboard that in a station
used to indicate the name of a town, no one knows anymore which
   one,
another watches over three lilies that wait in vain for a horseman,
but the last one tells me I'll come back to be inside a song of
   another century
and I'll return to hand over to a girl the coin I owe her.

Bajo el cielo nacido tras la lluvia

Bajo el cielo nacido tras la lluvia
escucho un leve deslizarse de remos en el agua,
mientras pienso que la felicidad
no es sino un leve deslizarse de remos en el agua.
O quizás no sea sino la luz de un pequeño barco,
esa luz que aparece y desaparece
en el oscuro oleaje de los años
lentos como una cena tras un entierro.

O la luz de una casa hallada tras la colina
cuando ya creíamos que no quedaba sino andar y andar.
O el espacio del silencio
entre mi voz y la voz de alguien
revelándome el verdadero nombre de las cosas
con sólo nombrarlas: "álamos", "tejados".
La distancia entre el tintineo del cencerro
en el cuello de la oveja al amanecer
y el ruido de una puerta cerrándose tras una fiesta.
El espacio entre el grito del ave herida en el pantano,
y las alas plegadas de una mariposa
sobre la cumbre de la loma barrida por el viento.

Eso fue la felicidad:
dibujar en la escarcha figuras sin sentido
sabiendo que no durarían nada,
cortar una rama de pino
para escribir un instante nuestro nombre en la tierra húmeda,
atrapar una plumilla de cardo
para detener la huída de toda una estación.

Así era la felicidad:
breve como el sueño del aromo derribado,
o el baile de la solterona loca frente al espejo roto.
Pero no importa que los días felices sean breves
como el viaje de la estrella desprendida del cielo,

Under the Sky Born after the Rain

Under the sky born after the rain
I listen to a gentle glide of oars in the water,
while I think that happiness
is no more than a gentle glide of oars in the water.
Or perhaps it's no more than a small boat's light,
that light that appears and disappears
on the dark wave-pattern of years
slow as a supper after a burial.

Or the light of a house found behind the hill
when already we believed there was nothing left but to walk
    and walk.
Or the space of silence
between my voice and the voice of someone
revealing to me the true names of things
by simply naming them: "poplars," "rooftiles."
Distance between the clink of the bell
on the bellwether's neck at daybreak
and the sound of a door closing after a party.
Space between the cry of the bird wounded in the marsh,
and the folded wings of a butterfly
over the crest of the hillock swept by the wind.

That was happiness:
to trace meaningless figures in the frost
knowing they wouldn't last at all,
to cut a pine twig
to write our names for an instant in moist earth,
to trap a thistle plume
to stop the flight of a whole season.

Such was happiness:
brief as the felled acacia's dream,
or the crazy spinster's dance before the broken mirror.
But it doesn't matter that happy times are brief
as the journey of a star unfastened from the sky,

pues siempre podremos reunir sus recuerdos,
así como el niño castigado en el patio
encuentra guijarros para formar brillantes ejércitos.
Pues siempre podremos estar en un día que no es ayer ni mañana,
mirando el cielo nacido tras la lluvia
y escuchando a lo lejos
un leve deslizarse de remos en el agua.

Lluvia inmóvil

No importa que me hayas cortado siete espigas
yo he roto todos los espejos
he cerrado todas las ventanas
y estoy condenado a permanecer
inmóvil en este pueblo
donde entre la lluvia y la vida hay que elegir la lluvia
donde el Hotel lo he bautizado Hotel Lluvia
donde los plateados élitros de la Televisión
relucen sobre tejados marchitos.

Tú me dices que todo se recupera
y que mi rostro aparecerá
en un río que ya he olvidado
y hay un camino para llegar a una casa nueva
creciendo en cualquier lugar del mundo
donde nos espera un niño huérfano
que no sabía éramos sus padres.

Pero a mí me han dicho que elija la lluvia
y mi nuevo nombre le pertenece
un nombre que no puede borrar ninguna mano
sino la de alguien que me conoce más que a mí mismo
y reemplaza mi rostro por un rostro enemigo.

for we can always bring their memories together,
just as the boy punished in the courtyard
finds pebbles to form brilliant armies.
For we can always be in a day not yesterday or tomorrow,
gazing at the sky born after the rain
and listening from a distance
to a gentle glide of oars in the water.

Immobile Rain

It doesn't matter that you've cut me seven spears of wheat
I've broken all the mirrors
closed all the windows
and I'm sentenced to remain
immobile in this town
where between the rain and life you have to choose the rain
where I've christened the hotel Hotel Rain
where Television's silver-plated aerials
gleam above the faded rooftops.

You tell me everything comes around
and that my face will appear
in a river I've already forgotten
and there's a road to reach a new house
going up anywhere in the world
where an orphan boy waits for us
not knowing we were his parents.

But they've told me to choose the rain
and my new name belongs to it
a name no hand can erase
but the hand of someone who knows me better than myself
and replaces my face with the face of an enemy.

Ultimo día de vacaciones

El Waltham del abuelo cae en el lago
y muere su último tictaquear de plata.
Los hongos venenosos esperan la lluvia.
El atardecer vierte yodo
sobre las heridas de los tejados.

Las vendedoras de castañas han juntado dinero
para comprar levadura o un almud de carbón. Yo
preparo el Bachillerato. Pero sólo veo
la araucaria olfateada por el Lobo Estepario.

Sin embargo, en el Club la vida es verdadera:
se discute el precio de trigo,
el abogado recuerda su destreza al billar;
ebrio, el profesor de matemáticas
se declara a la niña del calendario,
un jubilado pregunta por el Diario Oficial.

Llueve sobre los hongos venenosos, sobre castillos
de madera podrida. Pero el tren anuncia silbando
que nos llevará hacia el Norte, hacia el verano.

En el mes de los zorros

"My dreams are of a field afar
And blood and smoke and shot . . ."
                    —A. E. Housman

En el mes de los zorros
En el mes de los días de sol frío
Los ancianos que habían abandonado sus ojos a las tinieblas vieron
    a las montañas ebrias mirarlos fijamente y luego disolverse como
    relojes de arena.
Es otro sol el que se anunció con el ruido reluciente de los cuchillos
    en la cocina
que despertaron buscando las gargantas de las aves de los brezales.

Last Day of Vacation

Grandfather's Waltham falls into the lake
and its final silvery tic-toc dies.
Poison mushrooms wait for rain.
Afternoon pours iodine
over the rooftops' wounds.

The chestnut vendors have collected money
to buy yeast or a peck of coal. I
prepare for graduation. But all I see
is Steppenwolf sniffing the Norfolk Pine.

Nevertheless, in the Club, life is real:
they discuss the price of wheat,
the lawyer recalls his skill at billiards;
tipsy, the mathematics teacher
declares his love to the calendar girl,
a retiree inquires about the Official Newspaper.

It rains on the poison mushrooms, on castles
of rotted wood. But the train announces whistling
that it will carry us North, toward summer.

In the Month of Foxes

*"My dreams are of a field afar
And blood and smoke and shot . . ."*
                    —A. E. Housman

   In the month of foxes
In the month of days of cold sun
The old men who'd abandoned their eyes to the shadows saw the
   drunken mountains stare hard at them and then dissolve like
   hourglasses.
It's another sun that announced itself with the brilliant clatter of
   kitchen knives
that woke up looking for the throats of moorhens.

El pozo familiar cerró su boca
acallando las ranas parientas de aquellas con que
    jugábamos con los rústicos en las cantinas.
Y llegaron las hechiceras a reanimar los fríos
    braseros de la nevazón de los ciruelos.

    Quién nos devolverá los amigos muertos
ese mes de los zorros y los días de sol frío
después que los ancianos olvidaron sus juegos en el pozo y
    hundieron sus cuchillos
en la garganta de los pájaros descubridores de la ventana por donde
    no entra la noche.

    Quién nos devolverá
esa calle que ahora los ancianos vigilan airados
porque no pueden extirpar la zarza de ardientes raíces,
porque el viento mueve las hojas del bosque predicando esperanza
mientras las hechiceras remueven en sus calderos
la sangre de sus víctimas que beben friolentas porque ningún sol
    cantará en sus oídos.

    Grande fue nuestra caída
    bajo la burla de los zorros y el sol frío
deslumbrados por las hechiceras de grandes pechos blancos.
    Insomnes oíamos el rechinar de la horca,
nuestro amigo el grillo no cuidaría nuestras tumbas.

    Pero las hechiceras nada pudieron
contra el ciruelo inmaculado de la casa que incendiaron y sus petalos
    caídos formaron la alfombra
que enviaremos a los viajeros inesperados del retorno mientras los
    ancianos de nuevo se hundirán en un pozo que el cielo no conoce
sin dejar una sombra que legar a sus nietos que sólo se acordarán de
    nosotros que nunca dejamos de escuchar a los bosques secretos
predicando libertad con cada una de sus hojas.

The family well closed its mouth
hushing up frogs kin to those with which we played
    with country boys in the saloons.
And sorceresses arrived to rekindle the cold braziers of the plum
    trees' snowfall.

Who will return dead friends to us
that month of foxes and days of cold sun
after the old men forgot their games in the well and plunged their
    knives
into the throats of birds who discovered the window through
    which night does not enter.

Who will return to us
that street the old men now watch over, indignant
because they can't eradicate the bramble with fiery roots,
because wind stirs the forest's leaves preaching hope
while the sorceresses stir in their cauldrons
the blood of their victims they drink chilled because no sun will
    sing in their ears.

Great was our fall
    under the ridicule of foxes and cold sun
dazzled by sorceresses with great white breasts.
    Sleepless we heard the noose's creak,
our friend the cricket wouldn't tend our graves.

But the sorceresses could do nothing
against the immaculate plum tree of the house they set afire, and
    its fallen petals formed the carpet
that we'll send to unexpected travelers on their return, while the
    old men will once again sink into a well the sky has no
    acquaintance with
leaving no shadow to bequeath to their grandchildren who will
    remember of us only that we never stopped listening to the
    secret forests
preaching freedom with every one of their leaves.

Paisaje de Clínica

a Rolando Cárdenas

Ha llegado el tiempo
En que los poetas residentes
Escriban acrósticos
A las hermanas de los maníaco-depresivos
Y a las telefonistas.

Los alcohólicos en receso
Miran el primer volantín
Elevado por el joven psicópata.

Sólo un loco rematado
Descendiente de alemanes
Tiene permiso para ir a comprar "El Mercurio".

Tratemos de descifrar
Los mensajes clandestinos
Que una bandada de tordos
Viene a transmitir a los almendros
Que traspasan los alambres de púa.

William Gray, marino escosés,
Pasado su quinto delirium
Nos dice que fue peor el que sufrió en el Golfo Pérsico
Y recita a Robert Burns
Mientras el "Clanmore", su barco, ya está en Tocopilla.

From *Pequeña confesión*
(Small Confession)
(1978)

Clinical Landscape

To Rolando Cárdenas

The time has come
When the poets in residence
Write acrostics
To the sisters of manic-depressives
And to the telephone operators.

The alcoholics in withdrawal
Gaze at the first kite
Flown by the young psychopath.

Only one hopeless madman
Descendant of Germans
Has permission to go buy *El Mercurio*.

Let's try to decipher
The clandestine messages
That a flock of thrushes
Comes and transmits to the almond trees
That grow through the barbed wire.

William Gray, Scottish seaman,
His fifth delirium ended,
Tells us that the one he suffered in the Persian Gulf was worse
And he recites Robert Burns
While his ship, the *Clanmore*, is already docked at Tocopilla.

Ha llegado el tiempo
En que de nuevo se obedece a las campanas
Y es bueno comprar coca-cola
A los Hermanos Hospitalarios.

El Pintor no cree
En los tréboles de cuatro hojas
Y planea su próximo suicidio
Herborizando entre yuyos donde espera hallar cannabis
Para enviarla como tarjeta de Pascua
A los parientes que lo encerraron.

Los caballos aran preparando el barbecho.
En labor-terapia
Los mongólicos comen envases de clorpromazina.

Saludo a los amigos muertos de cirrosis
Que me alargan la punta florida de las yemas
De la avenida de los ciruelos.

La Virgen del Carmen
Con su sonrisa de yeso azul
Contempla a su ahijado
Que con los nudillos rotos
Dormita al sol atiborrado de Valium 10.

(En el Reino de los Cielos
Todos los médicos serán dados de baja).

Aquí por fin puedes tener
Un calendario con todos los días
Marcados de rojo
O de blanco.

Es la hora de dormir—oh abandonado—
Que junto al inevitable crucifijo de la cabecera
Velen por nosotros
Nuestra Señora la Apomorfina
Nuestro Señor el Antabus
El Mogadón, el Pentotal, el Electroshock.

The time has come
In which once again one obeys the bells
And it's good to buy Coca-Cola
From the Brothers Hospitaler.

The Painter doesn't believe
In four-leaf clovers
And he plans his next suicide
Botanizing among the weeds where he hopes to find cannabis
To send as a Christmas card
To the relatives who committed him.

The horses plow, preparing the fallow land.
In work therapy
The mongoloids eat packets of Chlorpromazine.

I salute friends dead of cirrhosis
Who extend to me the blossoming tips of their fingers
From the avenue of plum trees.

The Virgin of Carmen
With her blue plaster smile
Contemplates her godson
Who with his broken knuckles
Dozes in the stuffed woolen sun of Valium 10.

(In the Kingdom of Heaven
All the doctors will be dropped from the lists.)

Here at last you can have
A calendar with all the days
Marked in red
Or in white.

It's time for sleep—oh abandoned one—
For next to the inevitable crucifix at the head of the bed
May they watch over us
Our Lady Apomorphine
Our Lord Antabuse
Mogadone, Pentothal, Electroshock.

Mi amor por ti

Mi amor por ti
Es un vidrio roto por el mal alumno del curso
Una capilla con techo de zinc bajo la lluvia de Vilcún
Una manzana ofrecida a la profesora por el alumno bueno del curso
El viento sur jugando ajedrez contra el viento norte para decidir qué
     tiempo va a haber
La conversación con los mapuches que desde la costa traen las
     estrechas carretas de cochayuyo
El abejorro que zumba deslumbrado al contemplarse en el espejo
El olor a café en el molinillo de la tía solterona
El recuerdo de rostros bellos como las proas de los veleros de otro
     siglo que se recuerdan junto a la cocina económica
El encanto de leer el "Ojo" y recitar las tablas de multiplicar
El gallo de pelea cuyas heridas cura tu padre tras su última victoria
El maqui de los mendigos que aún no soporta el aliento de los
     camiones
El gesto del loco tratando de atrapar un rayo de sol con su sombrero
     en medio de la plaza
Un viaje en carreta con los primos para celebrar en la hijuela familiar
     el Año Nuevo
Las chispas de la locomotora a vapor iluminando la noche frente a
     mi perdida casa
Los nombres de poetas amados que repasamos como las cuentas de
     un racimo de uvas de Italia
El primer surco trazado por los colonos con sus arados de madera
Y en fin
La llave que se nos ha dado para unir la memoria con el olvido
Y que lanzo al fondo de un pozo
Para que alguien tan afortunado como nosotros hoy día la encuentre
     algún día.

My Love for You

My love for you
Is a window broken by the bad student in the class
A chapel with a zinc roof under the rain of Vilcún
An apple offered to the teacher by the good student in the class
The south wind playing chess with the north wind to decide what
    the weather will be
Conversation with the Mapuches who bring from the coast their
    narrow ox-carts full of kelp
The bumblebee that buzzes dazzled at viewing itself in the mirror
The smell of coffee in the grinder of the maiden aunt
The memory of pretty faces like the prows of sailing ships from
    another century remembered next to the wood stove
The enchantment of reading the ABC's and reciting the
    multiplication tables
The fighting cock whose wounds your father heals after its final
    victory
The beggars' blackcurrant bush that still can't tolerate truck
    exhaust
The grimace of the madman trying to trap a ray of sun with his hat
    in the middle of the plaza
A journey by ox-cart with the cousins to celebrate the New Year on
    the family estate
Sparks from the steam locomotive lighting up the night in front of
    my long-lost house
The names of beloved poets we repeat like beads from a bunch of
    Italian grapes
The first furrow traced by the colonists with their wooden ploughs
And finally
The key that's been given to us to join memory with forgetting
And which I hurl to the bottom of a well
So that someone as fortunate as we are today will someday come
    upon it.

Notas sobre el último viaje del autor a su pueblo natal

A Stefan Baciu en Hawaii,
y a Vasile Igna, mi primo desconocido,
en Cluj, Transilvania.

1

En el pueblo
donde algunos me conocen
como el poeta cuyo nombre suele aparecer en los diarios,
paseo por la Calle Comercio
que ahora se llama Avenida Bernardo O'Higgins
(como en Santiago).

He comulgado con la tierra.
Voy a la Sidrería.
Allí están los parroquianos de siempre
y me saludan mis viejos compañeros de curso
que sueñan con ser alcaldes o regidores o comprarse una citroneta.
Ha cerrado el cine.
Aún quedan affiches que anuncian películas de sepia.
A lo largo de los cercos
las ortigas siguen hablando con su indestructible lenguaje.
En el techo de mi casa se reúne el congreso de los gorriones.
Pienso por primera vez
que no pertenezco a ninguna parte,
que ninguna parte me pertenece.

Notas sobre el último viaje del autor
a su pueblo natal
(Notes on the Author's Last Journey
to the Town of His Birth)
(1978)

Notes on the Author's Last Journey to the Town
of His Birth

To Stefan Baciu in Hawaii,
and to Vasile Igna, my unknown cousin
in Cluj, Transylvania

I

In the town
where some know me
as the poet whose name appears regularly in the papers,
I walk down Commerce Street
which is now called Bernardo O'Higgins Avenue
(like the one in Santiago).

I have communed with the earth.
I go to the Cider Mill.
The regulars are there as always
and my old classmates greet me,
those who dream of being mayors or aldermen or of buying a
    Citronette.
The movie theatre has closed.
Posters announcing films in sepia still remain.
Along the fences
nettles go on speaking in their indestructible tongue.
On the roof of my house, the congress of sparrows convenes.
For the first time I think
that I don't belong to any place,
that no place belongs to me.

2

El viento trae olor a terneros mojados.

3

Kilómetro 662 a las cuatro de la tarde.
En la Calle Comercio los turcos y los españoles bostezan tras los
  mostradores.
No hay un alma en la calle a la hora de la siesta
horadada sólo por el cuerno primitivo del vendedor de helados.
En las afueras los campesinos esperan las micros rurales.
Tal vez me vaya a otro pueblo
cuyo destino voy a leer en la palma de sus calles.

4

Hay praderas manchadas de vacas y girasoles.
De las cosas que puedan consolarme cuando vuelva a la ciudad
  enferma de smog.
Viajaré en vagones de segunda atestados como los de las novelas
  sobre la Revolución Rusa.
He visto las ventanas ciegas del Molino.
Con su arruinado dueño he tomado un trago en cualquier cantina.
Paso la tarde sin darme el trabajo de llegar ni siquiera al fondo del
  patio de la casa paterna.

5

El único hojalatero que quedaba en el pueblo
fue a buscar trabajo a Lonquimay.
No ganó mucha plata pero contempló la Cordillera.
El no tiene Leica ni Kodak
así que se dedicó a dibujarla
para que sus nueve hijos la conocieran de verdad.

6

A los mapuches les gustan las canciones mexicanas del Wurlitzer de
  la única Fuente de Soda.
Las escuchan sentados en la cuneta de la Calle Principal.
Van a la vendimia en Argentina y vuelven con terno azul y
  transistores.
Ha llegado la TV.
Los niños ya no juegan en las calles.

2
Wind brings the smell of wet calves.

3
Kilometer 662 at four in the afternoon.
On Commerce Street the Turks and Spaniards yawn behind the
   display cases.
There's not a soul in the street at the hour of siesta
pierced only by the primitive horn of the ice-cream vendor.
On the outskirts the peasants wait for the rural busses.
Maybe I'll go to another town
whose destiny I'll read in the palms of its streets.

4
There are meadows splotched with cows and sunflowers.
Of the things which can console me when I return to the city sick
   with smog.
I'll travel in second-class cars like those in novels about the
   Russian Revolution.
I've seen the blind windows of the Mill.
I've had a drink with its ruined owner in some saloon or other.
I pass the afternoon without taking the trouble to go even to the
   end of the courtyard of my father's house.

5
The only tinsmith left in town
went to Lonquimay to look for work.
He didn't make much money but he gazed at the Mountains.
He's got no Leica or Kodak
so he devoted himself to drawing them
so that his nine children would truly know them.

6
The Mapuches like Mexican songs on the Wurlitzer in the only
   Soda Fountain.
They listen sitting on the curb on Main Street.
They go to the grape harvest in Argentina and return with blue
   suits and transistors.
TV has arrived.
Children no longer play in the streets.

Sin hacer ruido se sientan en el living para ver a Batman o películas
   del Far West.
Mis amigos están horas y horas frente a la pantalla.

Tengo ganas de que lleguen los Ovnis.

7
Me cuesta creer en la magia de los versos.
Leo novelas policiales,
revistas deportivas, cuentos de terror.
Sólo soy un empleado público como consta en mi carnet de
   identidad.
Sólo tengo deudas y despertares de resaca donde hace daño hasta el
   ruido del alka seltzer al caer al vaso de agua.
En la casa de la ciudad no he pagado la luz ni el agua.
Sigo refugiado en los mesones,
mirando los letreros que dicen "No se fía".
Mi futuro es una cuenta por pagar.

8
Si el futuro pudiera extenderse pulcramente
como mi madre extiende las sábanas de mi cama.
Miro la ropa puesta a secar en el patio.
Han entrado ladrones de gallinas a la casa del frente.
Voy a la plaza a leer el diario con noticias más añejas que las de San
   Pablo.

9
Solitario donde nunca he estado solitario
camino hasta el abandonado velódromo de tierra
donde no aparece ni el fantasma del Campeonato de Ciclismo de
   Chile del año 30.
Hay caballos pastando en lo que fue cancha de fútbol.
Todos se interesan sólo por ir a ver los partidos profesionales a la
   Capital de Provincia
mientras yo pienso mordisquear una brizna de brezo.

Making no noise they sit in the living room to watch Batman or
    films of the Far West.
My friends spend hours and hours in front of the screen.

I want the UFO's to arrive.

7
I have trouble believing in the magic of verse.
I read police novels,
sports magazines, tales of terror.
I'm merely a public employee as noted on my ID card.
I merely have debts and wake up with hangovers where even the
    sound of an Alka-Seltzer dropping into a glass of water hurts.
In the house in the city I haven't paid the light or the water.
I go on seeking refuge in taverns,
gazing at the signs that say "No credit given."
My future is a bill to be paid.

8
If only the future could be spread out neatly,
as my mother spreads the sheets on my bed.
I look at the clothing put out to dry in the courtyard.
Chicken thieves have broken into the house across the street.
I go to the square to read the paper with news more stale than
    stories of Saint Paul.

9
Lonely where I've never been lonely
I walk to the abandoned dirt velodrome
where even the ghost of the Chilean Cycling Championship of
    1930 doesn't appear.
There are horses grazing on what was a soccer field.
Everyone's interested only in going to see the professional teams in
    the Capital of the Province
while I think of nibbling a sprig of heather.

10

Trasnochador empedernido
contemplo la luna igual a la de 1945
enrojecida por la erupción del Llaima.
La misma que miraba desde la buhardilla
mientras leía como ahora "Los miserables" y el Almanaque
    Hachette.

11

Acuérdate que te recuerdo.
Si no te acuerdas no importa mucho.
Siempre te veré caminando sobre los rieles
o buscando el durazno más maduro de la quinta.

12

Ya pasó el Rápido a Puerto Montt
que antes se llamaba el Flecha del Sur.
Voy de la estación al puente
cuyos faroles dicen "Fundición Dickinson, 1918".
Ya no existe esa fundición
ni ninguna fundición.
Confío mi memoria al río Cautín y a la Capilla de Guacolda.
Afirmado en las barandas del puente
miro el cielo del verano que apenas sujetan los clavos de plata de las
    estrellas.

13

Hemos llegado a esta aldea en un Pontiac 40
por caminos que jamás serán pavimentados.
Espantamos cerdos y gallinas.
Los niños se asoman asombrados.
En el negocio clandestino
pedimos un pipeño y hablamos con el dueño
y con un tractorista que nos asegura que Hitler está vivo
y con dos recién llegados que nos convidan charqui de pescado:
son un estibador de Talcahuano y su compadre mapuche que lo trae
    al anca.
Todos bebimos en la misma medida,

10

Inveterate night-owl
I contemplate the moon just like the one of 1945
reddened by the eruption of Llaima.
The same one I gazed at from the garret
while I read as I do now *Les Misèrables* and the *Almanac
Hachette.*

11

Recall that I remember you.
If you don't recall, it doesn't matter much.
I'll always see you walking along on the rails
or looking for the ripest peach in the orchard.

12

The Express to Puerto Montt went by already
which was called the Southern Arrow before.
I go from the station to the bridge
whose lamps say "Dickinson Foundry, 1918."
That foundry no longer exists,
nor any foundry.
I entrust my memory to the Cautín River and the Chapel of
    Guacolda.
Steadied against the railings of the bridge
I gaze at the summer sky that the stars' silver nails scarcely hold in
    place.

13

We've arrived in this village in a 1940 Pontiac
along roads that will never be paved.
We frighten pigs and chickens.
Children peek out astonished.
In the speakeasy
we order new wine and talk with the owner
and with a tractor driver who assures us that Hitler is alive
and with two recent arrivals who treat us to fish jerky:
a stevedore from Talcahuano and his Mapuche pal he carries
    sidesaddle behind him.
We all drink at the same rate

y volvimos como nuestros antepasados
ebrios al pueblo que un día nos rechazará.

14
Día domingo de salida de misa.
Las niñas se pasean con la moda recién llegada de Santiago
acompañadas por la banda del Regimiento que toca cumbias.
Los dueños de casa compran las primeras sandías
y los diarios con las noticias frescas de los últimos crímenes.
Camino por las últimas calles de este lugar de bomberos, rotarios,
    carabineros, jubilados, tinterillos y profesores primarios,
allí los puñales del sol entran por las costillas de los pobres cercos de
    madera.
Siento los estertores de las postreras carretas y locomotoras a vapor.
Busco la paz tendiéndome en la pradera condecorada por los
    girasoles
contemplando el glorioso oleaje del trigo
y los viajes infinitos de las nubes que van a llorar por nosotros.

and we return like our ancestors
drunk to the town that will one day reject us.

14
Sunday morning after Mass.
Girls go by in the styles just arrived from Santiago
accompanied by the Regimental band playing *cumbias*.
Homeowners buy the first watermelons
and papers with fresh news of the latest crimes.
I walk through the outlying streets of this place full of firemen,
    rotarians, state police, retirees, shyster lawyers, and elementary
    school teachers;
daggers of sun come in there, through the ribs of poor wooden
    fences.
I feel the rattlings of the last ox-carts and steam locomotives.
I look for peace stretching myself out in the meadow decorated
    with sunflower medals
contemplating the glorious waves of wheat
and the infinite journeys of clouds that will weep for us.

Un día en Madrid

En Madrid la suerte está en manos de los ciegos.
En Madrid las mujeres se pintan las uñas de rojo
como las mujeres de las portadas del *Para Tí* que yo veía cuando mi
    madre me acompañaba al dentista.
Estoy en la calle La Gasca y frente al Bazkari donde voy a comer una
    sopa de pescadores
le doy limosna a una gitana que está orgullosa de tener un hijo con
    nombre de Rey Mago.

He comprado a un chamarilero la revista "Boxeo Mundial" de 1927
    en cuya portada aparece el Tani Loayza.
Voy de compras al Mercado de la Paz.
Converso en un estanco con un inválido de guerra.
Leo a poetas españoles que hablan de "la ciega presencia de la
    primavera" y de que "la mujer es una hucha".
Es invierno y me gusta ver a los niños vestidos como Toby y la
    Pequeña Lulú.

Qué raro es estar vivo en pleno Siglo XX
cuando se ama la luz de la nieve holandesa en el Museo del Prado.
Qué raro es estar sobrio
aún después de pasar por la Cervecería del Correo.
Podría estar horas frente a la vitrina de esa librería
donde se ve un reloj sobre una chimenea en cuya boca se interna
    una locomotora.

From *"Las ciudades que he conocido vivían como locas"**
("The Cities I Have Known Were Living Like Mad")*
(1978)

A Day in Madrid

For Jorge Edwards and Galvarino Plaza

In Madrid luck is in the hands of the blind.
In Madrid the women paint their fingernails red
like women on the covers of *Para Tí* which I saw when my mother
    went with me to the dentist.
I'm in La Gasca Street and in front of Baskari's where I'm going to
    eat fisherman's soup
I give alms to a gypsy woman who's proud to have a son named
    after one of the Three Wise Men.

From a second-hand dealer I've bought a copy of *World Boxing*
    from 1927 with Tani Loayza on the cover.
I go shopping in the Market of Peace.
I chat with a war invalid in a government store.
I read Spanish poets who talk of "the blind presence of spring" and
    of how "woman is a moneybox."
It's winter and I like seeing the children dressed as Toby and Little
    Lulu.

How odd it is to be alive in the middle of the 20th century
when light off the Dutch snow is loved in the Prado Museum.
How odd it is to be sober
even after walking through the Postal Brewery.
I could spend hours in front of the window of that bookstore
where a clock can be seen over a fireplace into whose mouth a
    locomotive rushes.

*Guillaume Apollinaire

Hay que viajar para no viajar.

En el ABC sólo leo los avisos económicos aunque no tenga nada que
    comprar,
y en la TV me intereso por el circo y los partidos donde juega
    Caszeli.

De nuevo aquí la noche podría ser mi mejor amiga.
Pero prefiero el atardecer donde los árboles sobrevivientes piensan
    en mí
y recuerdo los labios silenciosos de los cerezos de la Frontera.
Entro al Metro o a los cines sólo para dormir como en el vientre
    materno.
El polvo se acumula en mi máquina de escribir.
Estoy cansado de contar historias de provincia.
Enviaré postales lo más cursis posible diciendo que el único país
    donde me siento extranjero es mi país.
No iré a los toros ni al Museo de Cera.
No iré al Retiro a rendirle un minuto de silencio a Mallarmé.
Sigo leyendo historias de piratas que tenían razón de asaltar los
    galeones.
Me embriago con los últimos miradores y busco una flor para
    setenta balcones.

La calle se desangra en automóviles
cuando dos millones de madrileños parten fuera de la ciudad a
    celebrar la Pasión de Cristo.
Entre el estrépito de las bocinas
me doy cuenta
que aquí nadie puede estar "solitario como una montaña diciendo la
    palabra "Entonces"
y vuelvo a un silencio aldeano
quebrado sólo por el silbato lejano del afilador de cuchillos.

You have to travel so as not to travel.

In *ABC* I read only the classified ads even though I have nothing to
    buy,
and on TV I'm interested in the circus and the games where
    Caszeli plays.

Here again, night could be my best friend.
But I prefer late afternoon where the surviving trees think of me
and I recall the silent lips of cherry trees of the Frontier.
I go into the Metro or the movie theatres only to sleep as in my
    mother's womb.
Dust collects on my typewriter.
I'm tired of telling stories of the provinces.
I'll send the tackiest postcards possible saying that the only
    country where I feel like a foreigner is my own.
I won't go to the bulls or the Wax Museum.
I won't go to the Retiro to pay a moment of silence to Mallarmé.
I go on reading stories of pirates who were right to attack the
    galleons.
I grow giddy at the highest viewpoints and seek a flower for
    seventy balconies.

The street bleeds automobiles
when two million Madrilenians leave the city to celebrate the
    Passion of Christ.
Among the blaring of horns
I realize
that here no one can be "lonely as a mountain saying the word
    Then"
and I return to a village silence
broken only by the knife-grinder's distant whistle.

Los dominios perdidos

A Alain Fournier

Estrellas rojas y blancas nacían de tus manos.
Era en 189 . . . en la Chapelle d'Anguillon,
eran las estrellas eternas
del cielo de la adolescencia.
En la noche apagaste las lámparas
para que halláramos los caminos perdidos
que nos llevan hacia un laúd roto y trajes de otra época,
hacia una caballeriza ruinosa y un granero de fiesta
en donde se reúnen muchachas y ancianas que lo perdonan todo.

Pues lo que importa no es la luz que encendemos día a día,
sino la que alguna vez apagamos
para guardar la memoria secreta de la luz.
Lo que importa no es la casa de todos los días
sino aquella oculta en un recodo de los sueños.
Lo que importa no es el carruaje
sino sus huellas descubiertas por azar en el barro.
Lo que importa no es la lluvia
sino sus recuerdos tras los ventanales del pleno verano.

Te encontramos en la última calle de una aldea sureña.
Eras un vagabundo de barba crecida con una niña en brazos,
era tu sombra—la sombra del desaparecido en 1914—
que se detenía a mirar a los niños jugar a los bandidos,
o perseguir gansos bajo una desganada llovizna,

The Lost Domain

To Alain Fournier

Red and white stars were being born from your hands.
It was in 189 . . . in the Chapelle d'Anguillon,
they were the everlasting stars
of the sky of youth.
At night you extinguished the lamps
so we could find the lost roads
that would carry us toward a broken lute and costumes from
    another era,
toward a ruined stable and a granary used for a party
where girls would meet old women who forgive everything.

For what matters is not the light we kindle day by day,
but the one we extinguish sometime
to keep the secret memory of light.
What matters is not the house of every day
but the one concealed in the turning place of dreams.
What matters is not the carriage
but its tracks discovered by chance in the clay.
What matters is not the rain
but its memory through the picture windows of high summer.

We met you in the last street of a southern village.
You were a wanderer with a growth of beard and a little girl in your
    arms,
it was your shadow—the shadow of the one who disappeared in
    1914—
who stopped to watch boys play bandits,
or chase after geese in a listless drizzle,

o ayudar a sus madres a desvainar arvejas
mientras las nubes pasaban como una desconocida,
la única que de verdad nos hubiese amado.

Anochece.
Y al tañido de una campana llamando a la fiesta
se rompe la dura corteza de las apariencias.
Aparecen la casa vigilada por glicinas, una muchacha
leyendo en la glorieta bajo el piar de gorriones,
el ruido de las ruedas de un barco lejano.

La realidad secreta brillaba como un fruto maduro.
Empezaron a encender las luces del pueblo.
Los niños entraron a sus casas. Oímos el silbido del titiritero que te
    llamaba.
Tú desapareciste diciéndonos: "No hay casa, ni padres, ni amor;
    sólo hay compañeros de juego".
Y apagaste todas las luces
para que encendiéramos
para siempre las estrellas de la adolescencia
que nacieron de tus manos en un atardecer de mil ochocientos
noventa y tantos.

El retorno de Orfeo

In memoriam de Rosamel del Valle

La sangre blanca de un cerezo
era el anuncio de nuevas puertas.
Te marchaste junto al invierno
que con su lámpara desenreda las raíces
y hace surgir los sueños de los antepasados.
Viajas junto al invierno,
a las ardillas y a los pájaros nevados
que siempre recuerdan tus manos
alimentándolos en los parques transparentes.

or help their mothers shell peas
while clouds passed by like a stranger,
the only one who would truly have loved us.

Night falls.
And at the ringing of a bell calling us to the party,
the hard shell of appearances is broken.
The house watched over by wisteria appears, and a girl
reading in the gazebo beneath the chirping of sparrows,
and the noise of pulleys from a far-off barge.

The secret reality was gleaming like a ripe fruit.
They began to kindle the lights of the town.
Children went into their houses. We heard the whistle of the
    puppeteer who was calling you.
You disappeared telling us: "There is no house, nor parents, nor
    love; there are only the companions of our play."
And you extinguished all the lights
so that we could kindle
for all time the stars of our youth
that were born from your hands one afternoon in eighteen hundred
ninety-something.

The Return of Orpheus

In memoriam Rosamel del Valle

The white blood of a cherry tree
was the announcement of new doors.
You went away along with winter
that with its lamp untangles the roots
and makes the dreams of ancestors come forth.
You travel along with winter,
with squirrels and with birds of snow
that always recall your hands
feeding them in transparent parks.

La primavera quiso retenerte
para que descifraras una vez más
los jeroglíficos de sus ramas.
La primavera prometía en vano
el naranjo de la infancia en el patio de cemento
o transformaba en viñedo tu copa de vino.
Ya el tiempo había escrito "muerte" con tinta invisible.
Tu leías sus cartas
sabiendo que cada mañana uno debe despedirse de la muerte
diciendo "Hasta mañana".
"—Tu muerte o mi muerte—decías—serán como el derrumbarse
     fortuito de una lámpara".

Ahora el invierno ha recogido esa lámpara
y te ilumina en el viaje del retorno
hacia lo más profundo de la noche
lejos de donde la luz pueda alcanzarte.

Retrato de mi padre, militante comunista

En las tardes de invierno
cuando un sol equivocado busca a tientas
los aromos de primaveras perdidas,
va mi padre en su Dodge 30
por los caminos ripiados de la Frontera
hacia aldeas que parecen guijarros o perdices echadas.

O llega a través de barriales
a las reducciones de sus amigos mapuches
cuyas tierras se achican día a día,
para hablarles del tiempo en que la tierra
se multiplicará como los panes y los peces
y será de verdad para todos.

Desde hace treinta años
grita "Viva la Reforma Agraria"
o canta "La Internacional"
con su voz desafinada
en planicies barridas por el puelche,

Spring wanted to keep you
so you would decipher one more time
the hieroglyphics of its branches.
Spring promised in vain
the orange tree of childhood in the courtyard of cement,
or else it turned your cup of wine into a vineyard.
Already time had written "death" with invisible ink.
You read its letters
knowing that every morning one must say goodbye to death,
saying "Till tomorrow."
"—Your death or mine—you said—will be like the accidental
    toppling-over of a lamp."

Now winter has picked up that lamp
and lights you on your journey of return
toward the very depths of night
far from where the light could reach you.

Portrait of My Father, Militant Communist

On winter afternoons
when a mistaken sun gropes
for the acacia trees of lost springs,
my father drives in his 1930 Dodge
over the riprapped roads of the Frontier
toward villages that look like pebbles or flushed quail.

Or else he arrives through the mire
at the reservations of his friends the Mapuches
whose lands keep shrinking day by day,
to speak to them of the time when the earth
will be multiplied like the loaves and fishes
and will truly be for everyone.

From thirty years ago
he shouts "Long Live Agrarian Reform"
or sings the *Internationale*
in his off-key voice
upon flatlands swept by the *puelche* wind,

en sindicatos o locales clandestinos,
rodeado de campesinos y obreros,
maestros primarios y estudiantes,
apenas un puñado de semillas
para que crezcan los árboles de mundos nuevos.

Honrado como una manta de Castilla
lo recuerdo defendiendo al Partido y a la Revolución
sin esperar ninguna recompensa
así como Eddie Polo—su héroe de infancia—
luchaba por Perla White.

Porque su esperanza ha sido hermosa
como ciruelos florecidos para siempre
a orillas de un camino,
pido que llegue a vivir en el tiempo
que siempre ha esperado,
cuando las calles cambien de nombre
y se llamen Luis Emilio Recabarren o Elías Lafertte
(a quien conoció una lluviosa mañana de 1931 en Temuco,
cuando al Partido sólo entraban los héroes).

Que pueda cuidar siempre
los patos y las gallinas,
y vea crecer los manzanos
que ha destinado a sus nietos.

Que siga por muchos años
cantando la Marsellesa el 14 de julio
en homenaje a sus padres que llegaron de Burdeos.

Que sus días lleguen a ser tranquilos
como una laguna cuando no hay viento,
y se pueda reunir siempre con sus amigos
de cuyas bromas se ríe más que nadie,
a jugar tejo, y comer asado al palo
en el silencio interminable de los campos.

in clandestine labor union halls or locals,
surrounded by peasants and workers,
grade-school teachers and students,
barely a handful of seeds
from which the trees of new worlds could grow.

Honorable as a Castille cape
I remember him defending the Party and the Revolution
without hope of any recompense
just as Eddie Polo—his childhood hero—
fought for Pearl White.

Because his hope has been beautiful
as cherry trees blooming forever
at the side of a road,
I ask that he may live to see the time
he's always hoped for,
when the names of streets are changed
to Luis Emilio Recabarren or Elías Lafertte
(whom he met one rainy morning of 1931 in Temuco,
when only heroes went into the Party).

May he always be able
to raise ducks and chickens
and watch the apple trees grow
that he's destined for his grandchildren.

May he go on for many years
singing the *Marseillaise* on the 14th of July
in honor of his parents who came from Bordeaux.

May his days come to be peaceful
as a pool without wind,
and may he always be able to meet with his friends,
whose jokes he laughs at more than anyone,
to play horseshoes, and eat barbecue
in the interminable silence of the fields.

En las tardes de invierno
cuando un sol convaleciente
se asoma entre el humo de la ciudad
veo a mi padre que va por los caminos ripiados de la Frontera
a hablar de la Revolución y el paraíso sobre la tierra
en pueblos que parecen guijarros o perdices echadas.

1961

Despedida

> *". . . el caso no ofrece*
> *ningún adorno para la diadema de las Musas."*
> —Ezra Pound

Me despido de mi mano
que pudo mostrar el rayo
o la quietud de las piedras
bajo las nieves de antaño.

Para que vuelvan a ser bosques y arenas
me despido del papel blanco y de la tinta azul
de donde surgían ríos perezosos,
cerdos en las calles, molinos vacíos.

Me despido de los amigos
en quienes más he confiado:
los conejos y las polillas,
las nubes harapientas del verano,
mi sombra que solía hablarme en voz baja.

Me despido de las virtudes y de las gracias del planeta:
los fracasados, las cajas de música,
los murciélagos que al atardecer se deshojan
de los bosques de casas de madera.

Me despido de los amigos silenciosos
a los que sólo les importa saber
dónde se puede beber algo de vino,

On winter afternoons
when a convalescent sun
appears amidst the haze of the city
I see my father who drives over the riprapped roads of the Frontier
to speak of the Revolution and paradise on earth
in towns that look like pebbles or flushed quail.

1961

So Long

" . . . the case presents
No adjunct to the Muse's diadem."
—Ezra Pound

I say goodbye to my hand
that could point out the thunderbolt
or the quietness of stones
under the snows of old.

So they can be woods and sands again
I say goodbye to the white paper and blue ink
from which indolent rivers flowed,
hogs in the streets, empty mills.

I say goodbye to the friends
I've trusted most:
rabbits and moths,
the ragged clouds of summer,
my shadow that used to speak to me in an undertone.

I say goodbye to the virtues and graces of the planet:
the down-and-outers, music boxes,
bats that fall every afternoon like leaves
from the forests of wooden houses.

I say goodbye to silent friends,
those who only care to know
where you can drink some wine,

y para los cuales todos los días
no son sino un pretexto
para entonar canciones pasadas de moda.

Me despido de una muchacha
que sin preguntarme si la amaba o no la amaba
caminó conmigo y se acostó conmigo
cualquiera tarde de ésas en que las calles se llenan
de humaredas de hojas quemándose en las acequias.

Me despido de una muchacha
cuyo rostro suelo ver en sueños
iluminado por la triste mirada
de trenes que parten bajo la lluvia.

Me despido de la memoria
y me despido de la nostalgia
—la sal y el agua
de mis días sin objeto—

y me despido de estos poemas:
palabras, palabras—un poco de aire
movido por los labios—palabras
para ocultar quizás lo único verdadero:
que respiramos y dejamos de respirar.

and for whom all their days
are nothing but excuses
for crooning songs long out of style.

I say goodbye to a girl
who, without asking if I loved her or not,
walked with me and went to bed with me
any of those afternoons when the streets fill
with smoke of leaves burning in the ditches.

I say goodbye to a girl
whose face I often see in dreams
illumined by the sad glance
of trains departing under the rain.

I say goodbye to memory
and I say goodbye to nostalgia
—the salt and water
of my pointless days—

and I say goodbye to these poems:
words, words—a little air
moved through the lips—words
to conceal perhaps the only truth:
that we breathe and leave off breathing.

PART THREE

Poems from *Cartas para reinas de otras primaveras*
(Letters to Queens of Other Springs)
(1985)

Todo está en blanco

Todo está en blanco.
El alba reina en el reloj de pared.
Sus agujas se han detenido.
La sangre de mis venas es un lago en deshielo
	una muchacha se ahogaría al cruzarlo.

Mi doble viste de negro
y sonríe.
Cuando él ocupe mi lugar
bajará la escalera de caracol
y se pondrá esos guantes
que el Príncipe de la Mentira entrega a sus discípulos
para que puedan estrangularse
sin la ayuda de los extranjeros que los traicionaron,
frente al espejo que les sonríe por última vez
diciéndoles que creyeron ser bellos tenebrosos
mientras se oye el aplauso de sus admiradores
los blancos pájaros que vaciaron mis ojos
	y detuvieron el fluir de mi sangre
y luego parten en busca de mis únicos amigos
	aquellos que no conocen todavía el blanco
para decirle que cumplieron una misión más
	a su madre
la Gran Esfinge Blanca.

Ahora que de nuevo

Ahora que de nuevo nos envuelve el Invierno
enemigo de los vagos y los ebrios,
el viento los arrastra como a las hojas del diario de la tarde
y los deja fuera de las Hospederías,
los hace entrar a escondidas a dormir hasta en los Confesionarios.

Conozco esas madrugadas
donde buscas a un desconocido y un conocido te busca
sin que nadie llegue a encontrarse

Everything's Gone White

Everything's gone white.
Dawn reigns in the wall clock.
Its hands have stopped.
The blood in my veins is a thawing lake
    a girl would drown when crossing.

My double dresses in black
and grins.
When he takes my place
he'll descend the spiral staircase
and pull on those gloves
which the Prince of Lies hands to his disciples
so they can strangle themselves
without the aid of the foreigners who betrayed them,
before the mirror which grins at them for the last time
telling them they fancied themselves gloomy beauties
while hearing the applause of their admirers
the white birds that emptied my eyes
    and halted the flow of my blood
and then they depart in search of my only friends
    those who still don't know white
to say they've completed one more mission
    to their mother
the Great White Sphinx.

Now That Once Again

Now that once again Winter envelops us
enemy of drifters and drunks,
wind drags them around like pages of the evening paper
and leaves them outside the Charity Shelters,
makes them sneak in to sleep even in the Confessionals.

I know those daybreaks
where you look for a stranger and an acquaintance looks for you
without anyone's managing to meet

y los radiopatrullas aúllan amenazantes
y el Teniente de Guardia espera con su bigotito de aprendiz de
nazi
a quienes sufrirán la resaca por no pagar la multa.

Ahora que de nuevo nos envuelve el Invierno
pienso en escribir
sobre los areneros amenazados por la creciente
sobre *un reo meditabundo*
que va silbando una canción,
sobre las calles del barrio
donde los muchachos hostiles al forastero
     buscan las monedas para el flipper
y los dueños del almacén de la esquina
esperan entumecidos al último cliente,
mientras en el clandestino
los parroquianos no terminan nunca su partida de dominó.

Ahora que de nuevo nos envuelve el Invierno
veo un farol transformado en santo por un nimbo de niebla
y los amantes desamparados
besándose apegados a los cercos.

Ahora que de nuevo nos envuelve el Invierno
pienso que debe estar lloviendo en la Frontera.
Sobre los castillos de madera,
sobre los perros encadenados,
sobre los últimos trenes al ramal.
Y vivo de nuevo
junto a *Pan* de Knut Hamsun lleno de fría luz nórdica
     y exactos gritos de aves acuáticas,
veo a Block errando por San Petersburgo contemplado por el
     Jinete de Bronce
y saludo a Sharp, a Dampier y a Ringrose jugándose en Juan
     Fernández el botín robado en La Serena.

Me han llegado poemas de amigos de provincia
hablando de *una gaviota muerta sobre el techo de la casa*
del *rincón más oscuro de una estrella lejana*
de *navíos roncos de mojarse los dedos.*

and the radio-patrol cars howl menacingly
and the Lieutenant of the Guard waits with his little moustache of
    an apprentice
                     Nazi
for those who'll suffer a hangover for not paying the fine.

Now that once again Winter envelops us
I think I'll write
about beachcombers threatened by the rising tide
about *a musing criminal*
who goes along whistling a song,
about the neighborhood streets
where boys hostile to the outsider
    look for coins to play pinball
and the owners of the corner store
wait numbly for their final customer,
while in the speakeasy
the regulars never finish their game of dominoes.

Now that once again Winter envelops us
I see a street lamp transformed into a saint by a nimbus of mist
and the godforsaken lovers
pressed up against the fences kissing.

Now that once again Winter envelops us
I think it must be raining on the Frontier.
On the castles of wood,
on the chained dogs,
on the last trains to the mineshaft.
And I live again
with Knut Hamsun's *Pan* full of cold Nordic light
    and the precise cries of waterbirds,
I see Block wandering through St. Petersburg contemplated by the
    Bronze Horseman
and I greet Sharp, Dampier, and Ringrose in Juan Fernández
    gambling away the booty stolen in La Serena.

Poems have arrived from friends in the provinces
speaking of *a dead gull on the roof of the house*
of *the darkest corner of a distant star*
of *warships hoarse from getting their fingers wet.*

Y pienso frente a una chimenea que no encenderé
en largas conversaciones junto a las cocinas económicas
y en los hermanos despojados de sus casas y dispersos por todo el
    mundo huyendo de los Ogros
esos hermanos que han llegado a ser mis hermanos
y ahora espero para encender el fuego.

Sin señal de vida

¿Para qué dar señales de vida?
Apenas podría enviarte con el mozo
un mensaje en una servilleta.

Aunque no estés aquí.
Aunque estés a años sombra de distancia
te amo de repente
a las tres de la tarde,
la hora en que los locos
sueñan con ser espantapájaros vestidos de marineros
espantando nubes en los trigales.

No sé si recordarte
es un acto de desesperación o elegancia
en un mundo donde al fin
el único sacramento ha llegado a ser el suicidio.

Tal vez habría que cambiar la palanca del cruce
para que se descarrilen los trenes.
Hacer el amor
en el único Hotel del pueblo
para oír rechinar los molinos de agua
e interrumpir la siesta del teniente de carabineros
y del oficial del Registro Civil.

Si caigo preso por ebriedad o toque de queda
hazme señas de sol con tu espejo de mano
frente al cual te empolvas
como mis compañeras de tiempo de Liceo.

And in front of a fireplace I will not light
I think of long conversations next to wood stoves
and of brothers stripped of their houses and dispersed throughout
   the world fleeing from the Ogres
those brothers who have become my brothers
and whom I now await to light the fire.

No Sign of Life

Why give signs of life?
I could hardly send you a message
in a napkin with the waiter.

Even though you're not here.
Even though you're shadow years distant
I love you suddenly
at three in the afternoon,
the hour at which madmen
dream of being scarecrows dressed as sailors
scaring clouds in the wheatfields.

I don't know if remembering you
is an act of despair or elegance
in a world where in the end
suicide has become the only sacrament.

Perhaps I'd have to throw the switch at the crossing
to derail the trains.
Make love
in the only Hotel in town
to hear the water mills creak
and interrupt the siestas of the state police lieutenant
and the Civil Registry clerk.

If I'm thrown in jail for drunkenness or curfew violation,
make sun signals for me with the hand mirror
in which you powder your face
like my girlfriends from High School days.

Y no te entretengas
en enseñarles palabras feas a los choroyes.
Enséñales sólo a decir Papá o Centro de Madres.
Acuérdate que estamos en un tiempo donde se habla en voz baja,
y sorber la sopa un día de Banquete de Gala
significa soñar en voz alta.

Qué hermoso es el tiempo de la austeridad.
Las esposas cantan felices
mientras zurcen el terno único
del marido cesante.

Ya nunca más correrá sangre por las calles.
Los roedores están comiendo nuestro queso
en nombre de un futuro
donde todas las cacerolas
estarán rebosantes de sopa,
y los camiones vacilarán bajo el peso del alba.

Aprende a portarte bien
en un país donde la delación será una virtud.
Aprende a viajar en globo
y lanza por la borda todo tu lastre:
los discos de Joan Baez, Bob Dylan, los Quilapayún,
aprende de memoria los Quincheros y el 7° de Línea.
Olvida las enseñanzas del Niño de Chocolate, Gurdgieff
        o el Grupo Arica,
quema la autobiografía de Trotzki o la de Freud
o los 20 *Poemas de Amor* en edición firmada y numerada
        por el autor.

Acuérdate que no me gustan las artesanías
ni dormir en una carpa en la playa.
Y nunca te hubiese querido más
que a los suplementos deportivos de los lunes.

Y no sigas pensando en los atardeceres en los bosques.
En mi provincia prohibieron hasta el paso de los gitanos.

And don't amuse yourself
teaching bad words to the parrots.
Teach them only to say Papa or Mothers' Center.
Remember we live in a time when one must speak in an
   undertone,
and to sip the soup on an Awards Banquet day
means to dream aloud.

How lovely is the time of austerity.
Wives sing happily
while they mend the only suit
of their laid-off husbands.

Never again will blood run in the streets.
Rodents are eating our cheese
in the name of a future
where all the cooking pots
will overflow with soup,
and trucks will wobble under the weight of dawn.

Learn to behave yourself
in a country where accusation will be a virtue.
Learn to travel by balloon
and toss all your ballast overboard:
the records of Joan Baez, Bob Dylan, Quilapayún;
learn by heart the Quincheros, the 7° de Linea.
Forget the teachings of the Chocolate Boy, Gurdjieff,
      or the Arica Group;
burn the autobiographies of Trotsky or of Freud
or 20 *Poems of Love* in an edition signed and numbered
      by the author.

Remember that I don't like folk art
or sleeping in a tent on the beach.
And never could I have loved you more
than the Monday sports supplements.

And don't go on thinking about afternoons in the woods.
In my district they prohibited the gypsies from even passing
   through.

Y ahora
voy a pedir otro jarrito de chicha con naranja
y tú
mejor enciérrate en un convento.
Estoy leyendo *El Grito de Guerra* del Ejército de Salvación.
Dicen que la sífilis de nuevo será incurable
y que nuestros hijos pueden soñar en ser economistas
    o dictadores.

And now
I'm going to order another mug of *chicha* with oranges
and you
had better shut yourself up in a convent.
I'm reading *The War Cry* of the Salvation Army.
They say that syphilis will once again be incurable
and that our children can dream of being economists or dictators.

NOTES

Night Trains

The towns listed in section 15 are all on the rail line that runs through the provinces of Malleco and Cautín to the poet's home town of Lautaro. They are named in order from north to south.

The *puelche* is an icy wind that blows off the Andes Mountains across the plains and valleys of Chile.

Portrait of My Father, Militant Communist

The *Mapuches* are the native people of the South of Chile, called Araucanians by the Spanish. They were never conquered by the colonists' armies, but have lost much of their land and culture through economic exploitation and legal manipulation by the colonists' descendants. They continue to subsist on their reservations in the *zonas indígenas*, or on the outskirts of towns in Cautín, Malleco, and other southern provinces, where they earn cash as small traders or agricultural laborers.

The Castille cape is a heavy black woolen mantle or poncho worn in the rainy South of Chile, especially by railroad workers and *carabineros*, the national police.

Luis Emilio Recabarren was a legendary labor union organizer and newspaper publisher of working-class descent, who was active among the copper and nitrate miners in the North of Chile from the 1890's to the 1930's. He was a founder of the Chilean Communist Party.

Elías Lafertte Gaviño was a labor leader in the North of Chile in the generation preceding Recabarren's.

Temuco is the capital of the province of Cautín, and a major trade and rail center. In the 1930's it was still a pioneer outpost of the Chilean *frontera*.

Clinical Landscape

El Mercurio is Chile's leading newspaper, generally Christian Democrat or conservative in its editorial policy. But from 1973 until the restoration of democracy, it supported the regime of military dictator Gen. Augusto Pinochet.

Germans were among the European colonists who settled in the South of Chile in the nineteenth century. Another wave of German refugees arrived after the collapse of Hitler's Third Reich, and many of these (and their descendants) still sympathize with or actively support neo-Nazi and right-wing extremist movements in the country, including those groups which in

1973 helped to overthrow the government of Salvador Allende and establish Pinochet's regime.

Tocopilla is a major port on the northern desert coast of Chile, serving the nitrate and copper mining industries.

The line *"Es la hora de dormir—oh abandonado—"* (It's time for sleep—oh abandoned one—) is an ironic variation on a well-known line (*"Es la hora de partir, oh abandonado"*) from Pablo Neruda's *"La canción desesperada"* in *Veinte poemas de amor y una canción desesperada.*

My Love for You

Vilcún is a small town on a spur rail line to the east of Temuco, province of Cautín.

A Day in Madrid

Para Tí was a very popular Argentine women's magazine in the 1940's and 1950's, with a wide circulation throughout Latin America.

Tani Loayza was a renowned Chilean boxer who in the 1920's competed in his weight division for the World Championship—a great feat in those days for an athlete from an obscure, distant country.

Notes on the Author's Last Journey to the Town of His Birth

Bernardo O'Higgins (1778–1842), son of an Irish immigrant to Peru, was the first president of Chile after it gained independence from Spain in 1818. His name has been given to the main street in Santiago and to main streets in many other Chilean cities.

Lonquimay and Llaima are volcanoes in the Cordillera del Sur, the southern reaches of the Andes, in the provinces of Malleco and Cautín, not far from the poet's native town of Lautaro.

Puerto Montt, the southernmost major port city before one reaches the largely unsettled Zona Austral, is still the southern terminus of Chile's long north-south railway system.

Talcahuano is the port just north of the major southern city of Concepción.

La cumbia is a style of dance music from the Caribbean coast of Colombia, now so popular throughout Latin America that it tends to displace local musical styles.

No Sign of Life

Quilapayún, the Quincheros, and the 7° de Linea were popular Chilean folk music groups, specializing in traditional indigenous material and in songs of social consciousness and protest. All of their recordings were banned in the first years of the military dictatorship of Augusto Pinochet, as were the works of all the other well-known cultural figures mentioned in the poem.

Most people hurriedly destroyed, burned, or buried such incriminating materials in the first days after the September 1973 military coup. It was risky even to keep copies of the books of Chile's world-renowned, Nobel Prize–winning poet, Pablo Neruda. After all, he was also a well-known Communist! Even his beloved *20 Poems of Love*, a very early and nonpolitical work, was not above suspicion.

The Arica Group was a cult meditation group similar to the EST movement in the U.S. The group was based in the northern Chilean port of Arica, and was active during the Allende years.

ABOUT THE POET

Jorge Teillier was born in 1935 in the small town of Lautaro, Province of Cautín, in the South of Chile, the same region where Pablo Neruda had spent his boyhood a generation earlier. This region, generally called *la frontera*, still represented, as it had for Neruda, the farthest reaches of civilization—a land of thick forests, heavy winter rainfall, and indigenous *Mapuche* people, who kept mostly to themselves, wearing their native garb and speaking their own language. The towns were divided in half by the railroad, which was still the only means of transport before the Pan American Highway was completed. Teillier is descended from small farmers and artisans; his father Fernando Teillier, whose own parents came from France to settle, was an agrarian reform activist and rural union organizer who went into exile after the military coup of 1973. Teillier attended schools in Lautaro and in the larger town of Victoria, then studied at the University of Chile in Santiago, where he received his degree in history and education. After a year of teaching, he joined the staff of the *Boletín de la Universidad de Chile*, and eventually became its director. He has spent much of his adult life in Santiago, and more recently divides his time between a house in the capital and a country home near the town of Cabildo, north of Santiago.

Teillier began writing poetry at the age of twelve. His first book, *Para ángeles y gorriones*, appeared in 1956. Others soon followed: *El cielo cae con las hojas* (1958); *El árbol de la memoria* (1961), which won both the Gabriela Mistral and the Santiago Municipal Prizes; *Poemas del País de Nunca Jamás* (1963); *Los trenes de la noche y otras poemas* (1964); *Crónica del forastero* (1968), which won the Crav Prize; *Muertes y maravillas* (1971); *Para un pueblo fantasma* (1978); and *Cartas para reinas de otras primaveras* (1985). Besides poetry, he writes reviews and literary articles for Chile's leading magazines and newspapers, and takes part in literary conferences and events throughout the country.

ABOUT THE TRANSLATOR

Carolyne Wright was born in Seattle, and attended Seattle University, in the Humanities Honors Program, and Syracuse University, where she received the degrees of Master of Arts and Doctor of Arts in English and Creative Writing. From 1971 to 1972, she held a Fulbright Study Grant to Chile, where she first encountered the poetry of Jorge Teillier. Four volumes of her own poetry have been published, including *Stealing the Children* (Ahsahta Press, 1978), *Premonitions of an Uneasy Guest* (Associated Writing Programs Award Series, 1983), and *From a White Woman's Journal* (Water Mark Press Award Series, 1985). Several other manuscripts are completed or in progress, including a prose memoir of the year she spent in Chile, *The Road to Isla Negra*, which won the 1990 PEN/Jerard Fund Award for a work in progress of nonfiction by an emerging woman writer. From 1986 to 1988, she lived in Calcutta on an Indo-U.S. Subcommission Fellowship; and from 1989 to 1991 she was in Dhaka, Bangladesh, on a Fulbright Senior Research Grant, to translate and prepare anthologies and individual collections of the work of contemporary Bengali women poets and writers. She has taught at Syracuse and St. Lawrence Universities, and at William Jewell and Whitman Colleges. She has won several awards for her poetry, including the Academy of American Poets Prize, the Pablo Neruda Prize from NIMROD, a New York State CAPS Grant, a Witter Bynner Foundation Grant, and the John Masefield, Celia B. Wagner, Cecil Hemley, and Lucille Medwick Memorial Awards from the Poetry Society of America. From 1991 to 1992, she was a Fellow of the Bunting Institute, Radcliffe College, completing the manuscript of *The Road to Isla Negra*, and preparing the anthologies of Bengali poetry and short fiction.

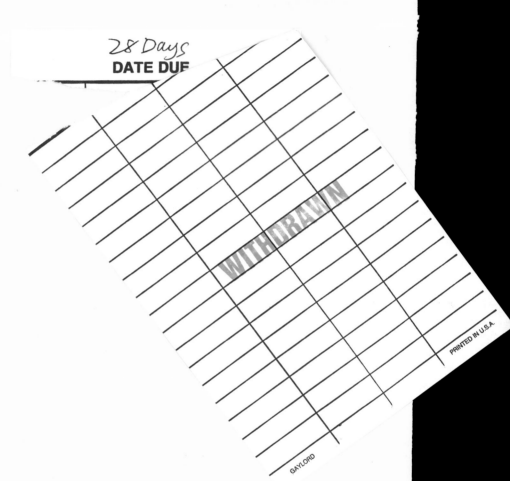

28 Days
DATE DUE

WITHDRAWN

PRINTED IN U.S.A.

GAYLORD